The Pilot's Guide To Preventive Aircraft Maintenance

The Pilot's Library General Editor, **Robert B. Parke**

FLYING AIRPLANES: THE FIRST HUNDRED HOURS BY PETER GARRISON
FLY ON INSTRUMENTS BY GEORGE C. LARSON
LONG DISTANCE FLYING BY PETER GARRISON
THE PILOT'S GUIDE TO PREVENTIVE AIRCRAFT MAINTENANCE BY J. MAC MCCLELLAN

Coming Soon:

WEATHER REPORT BY ROBERT B. PARKE
PILOT'S AVIONICS HANDBOOK BY GEORGE C. LARSON AND ROBERT DENNY

Other Doubleday Aviation Handbooks:

ANYONE CAN FLY BY JULES BERGMAN
PILOT'S NIGHT FLYING HANDBOOK BY LEN BUCKWALTER
THE PILOT'S GUIDE TO FLIGHT EMERGENCY PROCEDURES BY ALAN BRAMSON AND NELLIE BIRCH
FLIGHT TRAINING HANDBOOK BY THE FEDERAL AVIATION ADMINISTRATION

The Pilot's Guide To Preventive Aircraft Maintenance

by J. Mac McClellan

With Forward by
***Robert B. Parke,** General Editor*

A PILOT'S LIBRARY BOOK
DOUBLEDAY & COMPANY, INC.
GARDEN CITY, N.Y. 1982

Library of Congress Cataloging in Publication Data

McClellan, J. Mac.
The pilot's guide to preventive aircraft maintenance.

(A Pilot's library book)
Includes index.
1. Airplanes—Maintenance and repair. I. Title.
II. Series: Pilot's library.
TL671.9.M3 629.134'6
ISBN: 0-385-15105-5
Library of Congress Catalog Card Number 80–2865

Printed in the United States of America
First Edition

This book is dedicated to my father, T. T. McClellan, a very good mechanic.

Foreword

Not so many years ago most pilots equated turning their airplane over to an untried maintenance shop with going to the hospital for exploratory surgery. It made one sick just to think about it. These days a similar situation might make a pilot feel that he had given the shop foreman power of attorney for his checking account but if the shop was associated with a major airplane dealership or was one of the spanking new FBO and service facilities, he could feel some confidence that the work to be done would be completed as promised and on time.

Though any brush with general aviation maintenance can be traumatic, a dose of knowledge can have a soothing effect on any pilot about to hand his airplane over to the tender mercies of a maintenance shop. This book can help make the operation easier to swallow.

Regardless of the rules and requirements calling for inspections and record keeping most airplane owners have a compelling incentive to keep their flying machine airworthy, for few pieces of equipment can cause more trouble when not working properly. Pilots may grumble about government interference and bureaucratic paperwork but when it comes to caring for their engine and airplane most pilots would rather have the Federal Aviation Administration err on the side of conservatism rather than casualness. Airworthiness Directives from the FAA and

Service Letters from manufacturers may cause pilots to have anxious moments but it is generally understood that the alternatives could be worse.

To the manufacturer, the area of airplane maintenance and aftermarket care is known as service and support and it has been receiving a good deal of attention in recent years. One reason is that some manufacturers found that indifference to an owner's problems was making former owners of some pilots and brand switchers of others. It became apparent that an increasing number of airplane purchases were swinging on the reputation of the manufacturer for service and support after the airplane changed hands.

Parts availability in service centers has always seemed to be a serious problem in general aviation airplane maintenance. Horror stories of airplanes being grounded for months while awaiting the arrival of a simple part used to be as common as broken wrists among hanggliders. The situation is somewhat better now and most manufacturers have computerized inventory systems and overnight shipping facilities but there are still occasional throwbacks to the old days, when the words "We've ordered it from the factory—it will be a few days" would strike terror to the heart of an owner in need of his airplane.

A sign that times have changed may be gleaned from the fact that I can assure any owner that if he suspects he is getting less than the complete attention of a manufacturer-associated maintenance facility, he will not be put on hold if he calls the president of the company that built his airplane. He may get neither the part nor a solution to his problem but he will certainly get an explanation and a flurry of activity. Manufacturers these days are entirely conscious of the fact that with airplane prices as high as they are, every hour an airplane sits on the ground when an owner wants it in the air is not only money lost but the sense of disappointment at an expensive piece of machinery failing to deliver. This must be weighed when the time comes to think about the next airplane. As a result, in many areas there is vigorous competition between manufacturers to prove that they still love an airplane buyer even after he takes delivery.

Contributing to the more wholesome climate at first line maintenance facilities is the fact that A&P training schools and related engineering establishments have recently improved their facilities and strengthened their curriculums. While there are still some A&Ps coming on line through a system of apprenticeship, it's the graduates of the likes of Parks College with their clean fingernails and Bachelor of Science degrees that get first crack at the good jobs. And increasingly, general aviation maintenance facilities can compete with the airline and military in terms of twenty thousand dollar a year salaries and fringe benefits. For many graduates, the benefits of working regular hours and in pleasant surroundings at an FBO have been more attractive than the presumed stability of an airline job.

You will find that as you read this book the enthusiasm for pilots, no matter how agile and mechanically inclined, doing their own maintenance is muted. As you will see, the reason is that many of the tasks that can legally be done by airplane owners are also the jobs that do not cost a great deal to have done professionally. Then too there is always the awful risk that an enthusiastic amateur may leave undone what should be done and cause himself more harm than could be justified by his desire to be a part of the maintenance loop. There is also the probability that if the pilot handyman turns up something unforeseen, he will certainly have to call in a pro anyway. Therefore, the rule in this book is that if you have a relatively simple machine that you bought as much to tinker with as to fly, go ahead and enjoy yourself. But if you have an expensive, complicated, modern high performance, heavily used aircraft on which you depend for reliable safe transportation, pay your dues and play it safe. While having your maintenance done at a professional shop is no guarantee that mistakes won't be made, at least there is the very good chance that your work will be done correctly.

With that as a backdrop, let me add that a completely unofficial survey of mechanical failures in general aviation airplanes reveals that an extraordinarily high proportion of them took place shortly after an inspection or major maintenance. Pilots who assume that the airplane coming out of the shop is the airplane that is supremely airworthy are often pilots with regrets. The smart money is on the pilot who follows the maintenance shop visit with a microscopic preflight, a thorough run-up, and a few flights around the pattern before he launches on the long cross-country at night.

One pilot I know had his years of cautious postmaintenance

flying pay off when on the second trip around the patch his oil drain plug fell out, allowing him barely enough altitude and time to test his airplane's capability as a slippery glider. Happily, he made it safely back to earth. Another acquaintance tells of failing to eye his trim function after a maintenance stop. On takeoff, he learned to his surprise that the trim cables had been reversed and that his normal up trim was bringing him closer to the greensward. In time, he figured out his problem and landed safely.

For every tale of carelessness and oversight in the maintenance shop, there is another of prompt analysis and speedy repair, if one looks closely enough. I remember with satisfaction a Cherokee Six flight where my on-time arrival had a high priority as I was the speaker at a gala dinner. Several hundred miles short of the destination and with dusk falling, the ammeter needle slipped into discharge and my transmissions became unreadable. I landed at a small airport and found the Piper dealer tidying up, ready to go home. After hearing my story, he caught his mechanic on the way to his car and together they uncowled the airplane. As they suspected, the generator bolt was loose, allowing the belt to slip. In thirty minutes I was airborne with another story of how good some maintenance can be.

Another time my preflight caught a cracked exhaust stack at a lonesome airport where I'd landed for fuel. I remembered scanning the desolate western plains and scruffy-looking town on the approach and feeling grateful that my stay would be brief. With replacement stacks probably at least a couple of days away I was resigned to solitary. But the lineperson turned out to be an A&P and a master welder. He also was helpful and willing so that two hours later when I took off we were warm friends. The scruffy-looking town now seemed to be a lovely oasis that I was sorry to leave so soon.

While nothing can make downtiming an airplane more pleasant than flying it, this book can surely help airplane owners feel less anxious and be more understanding when they must consign their aircraft to the shop.

Robert B. Parke

Contents

Foreword *ix*

Introduction *xv*

1 ***A Guide to Scheduled Inspection and Maintenance*** *1*

2 ***How to Identify a Quality Maintenance Shop*** *26*

3 ***Maintenance Records: What's Required and How to Keep Them*** *36*

4 ***Preventive Maintenance an Owner-Pilot Can Legally Perform*** *45*

5 ***Major Engine Repair and Overhaul, the Most Expensive Part*** *100*

6 ***Airframe Problems You Can Expect and How to Solve Them*** *118*

7 ***Avionics and How to Keep Them Working and Make a Coherent Installation*** *129*

8 ***Airworthiness Directives and How to Deal With Them*** *142*

9 ***Safe and Saving Operating Techniques: The Best Way to Save on Maintenance Bills*** *150*

Index *161*

Introduction

Safety is the first priority in aviation, but for the light airplane owner operating costs are a close second. Fuel prices have grabbed the cost headlines of late but an average light airplane owner will spend nearly as much, and often more, for maintenance as for fuel.

For example, in 1980 Piper estimated that it would cost $11.35 cents for gas and oil for each operating hour in an Arrow. However, scheduled maintenance plus reserves for engine and prop overhaul were expected to cost $11.47 per hour. After investment expense, light aircraft maintenance can be the most costly part of airplane ownership.

There is no such thing as good cheap maintenance. Service can be cheap or good but will never be both. The object of this book is to point out how we can obtain and identify good maintenance which is also the most cost effective maintenance and certainly is the safest way to fly.

This book is divided into chapters detailing scheduled inspections and maintenance, engine maintenance, and other specific areas of interest. It is not essential to read the entire book at one time to benefit but rather you may simply read and then refresh your memory in the area of present interest.

There are many maintenance procedures airplane owner-pilots may legally perform themselves and I discuss the pros and cons of each of those preventive maintenance procedures. This is not a "how to" book because the specifics will vary for every airplane type, but there is enough information to help you decide if you should tackle a repair job yourself. For most pilots home maintenance is not cost effective because specialized tools, equipment, and skills are required. But if you do decide to take on an allowable maintenance task, service manuals published by the airplane manufacturer are the place to look for specifics.

Saving money on maintenance is the theme of this book and the way to save is by knowing what to look for and what to demand from your shop. The lowest price work may not be the highest in value but the repair job that delivers the most useful flight hours per dollar is. Chapters on how to identify a good shop, what to expect at major engine overhaul time, and how to deal with Airworthiness Directives will help you get the most for your money.

The Pilot's Guide To Preventive Aircraft Maintenance

1

A Guide to Scheduled Inspection and Maintenance

The captain is the captain. That old rule of the sea has carried over to even the smallest airplane we can fly. If you're the pilot, you're the captain of that airship and are held responsible for everything about that airplane—including its mechanical condition.

Our friends in the FAA are fond of making rules for us to fly by but they are very careful to avoid assuming any responsibility or even spreading responsibility around. There is only one facet of flying in which the FAA assumes a responsibility and that is for traffic separation under IFR. Even then there are many loopholes through which the FAA can pass the buck to the pilot should he fly into another airplane.

Most pilots are aware of their responsibility to fly the airplane according to the Federal Air Regulations (FARs). That lesson is drummed into all of us from the very beginning, but few pilots really stop to think that they are responsible for the airworthy condition of any airplane they fly. No matter who owns the airplane, the captain is still the captain and the responsibility is his.

During our earliest flight training, the instructor went over paperwork requirements, teaching us to look for proper documentation. The airworthiness certificate, registration, and so on, are all required for legal flight. And, there is also a requirement that the pilot determine whether or not the airplane has received all required maintenance inspections. For most of us that meant we checked to see if airframe and engine logs were present. We may even have looked inside the log to see when the 100-hour inspection was due but that was the extent of our brush with maintenance requirements.

The full impact of scheduled maintenance doesn't hit any pilot until that pilot becomes an airplane owner. Then it's a whole new ball game. I have often thought the real difference between flying my own airplane and flying one owned by someone else is my attitude toward mechanical problems. A funny noise from the engine or a glitch in the systems of any other airplane I am flying scares the hell out of me and I wonder if I'm going to crash. In my airplane strange noises from the engine or any other problems conjure up only one thought—what is this going to cost me.

Inspections and scheduled maintenance are going to cost a great deal. Next to engine overhaul or replacement, scheduled inspections are the biggest single expense in maintaining a light airplane.

It has been my experience and also that of many other light airplane owners that inspection costs are nearly immune to operational hours. Whether the airplane flies 100 hours a year or 500 hours a year, the annual inspection and the problems it reveals seem unrelated or at least do not increase in a linear fashion for hours of usage.

Much of the cost of an inspection goes into labor—labor needed to disassemble the airframe, check the engine, and so on. It is going to take just as much time to disassemble the airplane and perform an inspection if the airplane has flown only 50 hours since its last annual inspection or has flown 500. The point is, inspections account for a large share of maintenance expense and will not vary directly with usage, so budget for those inspections at about the same rate no matter how much you fly.

There are many required inspections that apply to airplane owners and we will cover all of those requirements in this chapter, but the place to start is with the inspection that gets us all—the annual inspection. Just as its name implies, the annual is required once every twelve months and must be completed by

Removing inspection plates and inspecting the vital components inside are a major part of an annual inspection. The inspection plate on the underside of the wing of a Cessna 337 shown here covers a fuel line connection. The inspector probably won't find anything wrong under the plate but a check must be made. The time it takes to remove all the screws, look inside, and refasten the plate adds to the labor cost of an annual.

the last day of the month in which the airplane was inspected the previous year.

The annual is carte blanche for maintenance shops. The rules are simple—everything on the airplane must be examined and approved by an authorized inspector (IA). The authorized inspector is a cut above the standard licensed aircraft mechanic, the A&P. A&P stands for airframe and power plant, and any work performed on an airplane, except for a specific list of procedures that can be accomplished by a pilot, must be signed off in permanent maintenance records by an A&P.

Like pilots, the A&P mechanic must pass a written test, complete a specific period of in-service training under licensed mechanics, and then finally pass an oral test given by the FAA. The

A&P designation means the mechanic is qualified to work on both engines and airframes. The FAA keeps those two areas separated in testing and training procedures and it is possible for a mechanic to be certified to work on engines but not airframes. However, most mechanics receive their licenses in both areas of maintenance.

Once a mechanic receives his A&P license he can begin working toward an inspection authorization rating. It takes several years of experience as an A&P plus more written and oral testing to receive the IA rating. Few mechanics progress to the inspector level and it is not uncommon for a shop to have several A&Ps working under a single authorized inspector.

Although the definition of a "complete inspection of the aircraft" is left to the authorized inspector you can be sure a good annual inspection is just that—complete. Every inspection plate on the airframe will be removed, every system checked and examined, and the engine gone over with a fine-tooth comb.

The complexity of an annual will vary according to the complexity of an airplane. Retractable landing gear add considerably to the annual bill because the airplane must be jacked up and the gear retracted. Worn bushings, improper alignment of gear doors, and looseness or wear in the landing gear retraction mechanism are common problems and are what the authorized inspector will be looking for. Sadly for our wallets, these problems often show up.

The engine is also a source of considerable expense and worry on the part of every owner at annual time. A complete inspection of the engine includes the equivalent of a "tune-up" and the dreaded compression test. If there is a major problem with the engine or it is simply wearing out, the compression test will reveal the problem.

To test compression all spark plugs are removed and a shop plug is placed in one of the two spark plug openings in a cylinder. Compressed air is fed into the cylinder through the other spark plug opening and a differential pressure gauge measures the amount of air pressure the cylinder is holding. Usually for most small light airplane engines the mechanic will set the compression tester for 80 pounds per square inch of pressure. A

The compression check is one of the most critical parts of any annual inspection. Compressed air is forced into each cylinder and a special differential pressure gauge measures the amount of pressure the cylinder is holding. Typically, the compression tester will be set at 80 pounds per square inch and the cylinder must hold at least 60 psi to pass the test. The compression test can quickly spot worn or cracked piston rings, worn cylinder walls, burned valves, or worn valve seats. Most engine problems are discovered during the compression test, making it one of the most threatening to an airplane owner's budget.

second gauge on the tester will show the actual pressure the cylinder is holding.

Whether a cylinder passes or flunks the compression check is up to the IA, but most inspectors will require the cylinder to hold 75 per cent of the pressure applied. That means if 80 pounds of pressure are forced in, the cylinder must hold at 60 pounds to pass the test.

Cylinders leak compression in three primary areas—around the piston rings, through the intake valve, or through the exhaust valve. If piston rings or cylinder walls are worn, the mechanic will listen to the oil filler spout and hear air rushing past the piston rings and into the crankcase. If no air is escaping into the crankcase but compression is low, the mechanic will listen to the exhaust pipe to check for air escaping out the exhaust valve. The final spot to check for low compression is the carburetor and if escaping air can be heard there the intake valve is leaking.

Worn piston rings or a worn cylinder wall are really bad news for the airplane owner. There is no solution but to pull the cylinder off the engine to determine the problem. Worn piston rings will often break, allowing compression to escape into the crankcase. Usually the cracked rings will perform their compression holding function when the engine is running but there is the danger that they will break into small pieces and fall into the engine where the metal fragments could do much damage.

If compression is leaking out either of the valves, most mechanics will try to "stake" the valve. Staking merely means the valve is rapped with a soft hammer and allowed to snap back against the valve seat. If a particle of carbon or other matter has lodged between the valve edge and the valve seat, this process often dislodges the object and allows the valve to seal.

The exhaust valve is the most common source of compression leaks because it operates at such high temperatures. The very hot exhaust gases flowing out around the edge of the valve under high pressure can burn the valve edge, causing it to leak. A burned valve edge or burned valve seat both require the same remedy—removing the cylinder for examination and replacement—and that is a very expensive procedure.

The mechanic who performs the compression check will often mark the compression value for each cylinder on the valve cover or at some other location in the engine area. If you see markings such as 80-72 written near or on a cylinder, you know that at some previous inspection that cylinder held 72 pounds of the 80 pounds pressure applied and that is good compression.

New engines will typically have good but not extremely high compression until the break-in period is complete. Once the piston rings have seated and the engine is through the break-in period you can expect new cylinders to hold all or nearly all of the 80 pounds pressure applied during a compression check.

The compression check is a vital part of all annual inspections because it can reveal impending problems that may lead to

Many mechanics will write the results of compression tests on the engine valve covers. You can see that this Cessna 182 engine passed its compression test with flying colors with the weakest cylinder holding 70 of the 80 pounds applied. Most inspectors will allow a cylinder holding as few as 60 pounds to pass an annual inspection.

a sudden engine failure and because low compression indicates reduced engine power output. New engines delivered from the factory under the guaranteed horsepower output program by Teledyne Continental and Avco Lycoming, currently the only major makers of light airplane engines in the United States, will have up to five per cent more power than rated horsepower but no less. That means an engine rated for 200 horsepower may put out 210 horsepower when new from the factory but in no case will deliver less than 200 horsepower. As the engine wears, and that wear is demonstrated by loss of compression, power output also drops. At some point, even though the engine is capable of running just fine, it simply won't put out enough power to pull the airplane safely off the ground. It is up to the authorized inspector at each annual inspection to determine when that point has been reached.

An even more immediate concern is to locate impending

problems in the engine that could cause it to stop in flight, forcing an off-airport landing. Worn valve stems, for example, which will show up in a compression check, could snap in flight and wreck the engine, not to mention ruining the pilot's whole day. As I noted, the compression check holds the most financial terror for an airplane owner at annual inspection time but it really is essential for a safe engine.

The "tune-up" phase of an annual engine inspection will include a complete examination of the ignition system from the magnetos to the spark plugs. There are two of everything in an airplane ignition system for redundancy which keeps you flying when one half of the system fails. But that redundancy also doubles the work of ignition inspection and adds the extra burden of aligning the two systems so they perform in harmony.

Airplane engines use magnetos to generate the electrical charge for spark plugs rather than the coil system used in automobiles because a magneto is independent of the battery and electrical system while a coil or transistor ignition system is not. If your battery fell out of the airplane, the magnetos would go right on doing their job although somebody on the ground would hate to see that battery fall through their roof. Magnetos are more expensive than a spark coil and require more maintenance but are the only means of providing ignition spark independent of the aircraft electrical system.

During the annual the magnetos will be checked for integrity to make certain they are firmly mounted to the case of the engine and no play has worked into the spinning magnets. As you probably know, magnetos generate electrical current by rotating one permanent magnet within the magnetic field of another permanent magnet. Breaker points are used to control the spark output and the spark is timed to fire by rotating the magneto base slightly on the engine case. A gear on the crankshaft of the engine drives the magnetos and other accessories.

Once the magnetos have been checked and timed the mechanic will examine the spark plug wires or harness, as it is called. The harness is vital for good transmission of the very high voltage current from magnetos to spark plugs. Also, the harness must contain the electrical current so completely that it does not interfere with the radios in the airplane. Often the wires in the

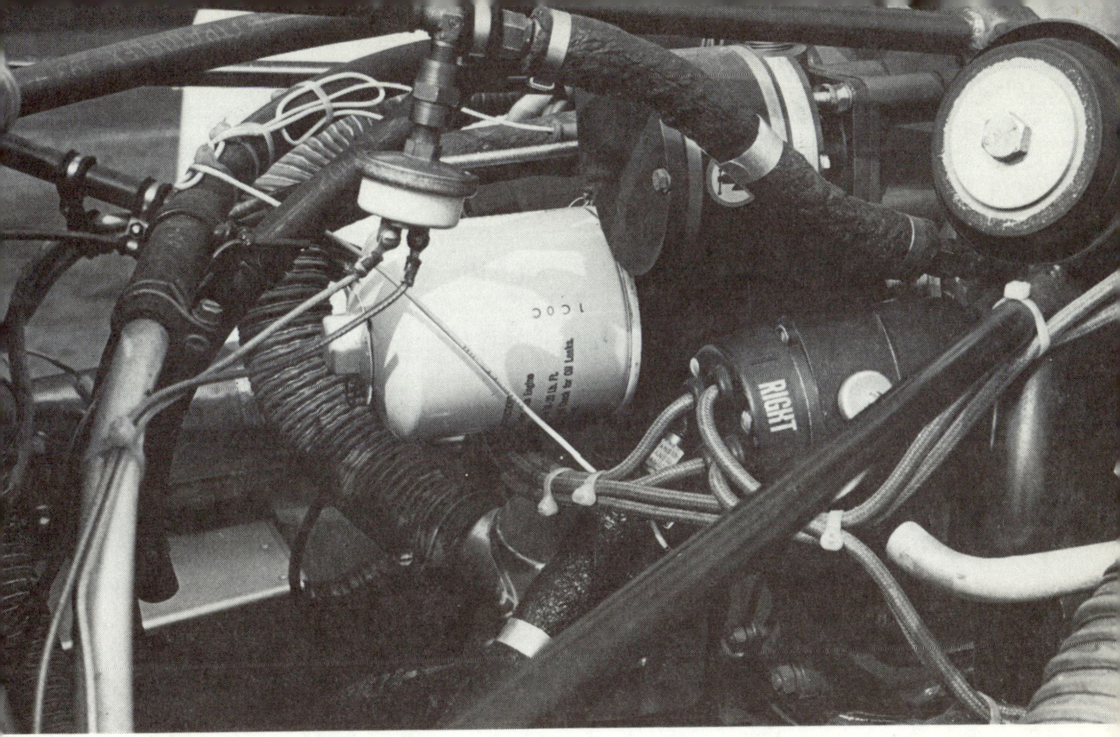

The right magneto is clearly visible on the rear of this Piper Archer engine. Magnetos are driven by gears within the engine and generate a powerful spark with each revolution. Right and left mags are of opposite electrical polarity and cannot be interchanged. As you can see, the position of this mag is clearly labeled on its housing.

harness are run through pipes to protect the wires from engine heat and chafe caused by vibration.

The harness wire terminates by screwing onto the top of the spark plug. A small porcelain insulator with a coil spring called a cigarette fits into the top of the plug and electrically connects the harness wire to the spark plug. All of these elements must be sound or electrical energy for the spark will be sacrificed. Even small flaws in the harness, cigarette, or the spark plug itself will allow high voltage electricity to escape, creating a very annoying popping sound in the airplane radios.

Aircraft spark plugs are expensive and demand special care. With such care they can last through hundreds of hours of service. A good mechanic will always arrange the spark plugs in a holder as they are removed to keep tabs on which cylinder each plug came from. After cleaning and visual inspection, the plugs will be rotated to the next cylinder in the firing order and moved from top to bottom cylinder hole to help even out electrode wear.

Visual examination of the spark plugs will tell the experienced mechanic a great deal about the quality of combustion in the cylinder a plug came from. The color, amount, and type of deposit on the plug and wear of the electrode all tell the expert what is going on inside that cylinder.

There are two major types of aircraft engine spark plugs—massive electrode and fine wire electrode. The massive electrode plug has a center electrode surrounded by two or three grounding electrodes which form nearly a complete circle around the center electrode. The fine wire plug has a smaller center electrode with two very fine wires approaching the center electrode from either side.

Fine wire spark plugs cost a great deal more because the fine electrode must be made from a platinum alloy. The platinum is needed to give the fine wires resistance to wear from spark

This mechanic is holding a fine wire spark plug (left) and a massive electrode plug (right). Notice how extremely fine the wire electrodes are in the left plug. These wires are made from platinum, which is one of the few metals hard enough to stand up to engine heat and wear. The open design of the fine wire plug helps prevent fouling from lead deposits and the hardness of the electrodes should provide 1,000 hours or more of service. The massive electrode plug is much like an automotive spark plug except it has more than one base electrode element. Massive electrode plugs should provide good service for 500 hours or more.

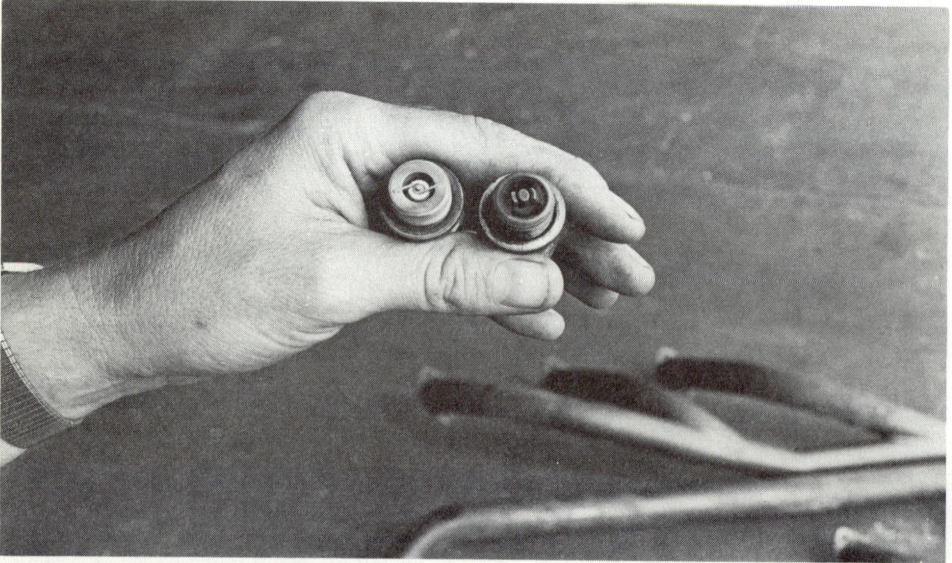

jump between electrodes. The fine wire plugs do wear very well and also resist fouling due to engine flooding because there is more room between electrodes in a fine wire plug. The only disadvantage is that fine wire plugs cost several times as much as massive electrode plugs.

The massive electrode plug will perform to total satisfaction but will not last as long. The question is, will the fine wire plug last enough longer to make up the price difference over a massive electrode plug? A good shop should be able to advise you on plug selection, taking into account how often you fly and how cold outside temperatures in your area are because the fine wire spark plug will have a cold starting advantage.

The fuel system and carburetor, if your engine has one, will also be carefully checked during an annual inspection. Worn lines, loose or leaking fittings, and fuel filters or screens will all be checked. In a carburetor the float level may require adjustment but that is not a frequent problem. Minimum idle speed is a more common adjustment but is not a big project.

Fuel injection systems require little in the way of regular maintenance. Either they work or they don't. Checking fuel filters, deck pressure—that is the fuel pressure at the junction of fuel lines to each cylinder—and general examination for fuel line integrity is the normal procedure. But when things go wrong a fuel injection system is typically much more expensive to repair than a carbureted system. Injector nozzles that deliver the fuel into the cylinders can plug up and may require cleaning or replacement. Fuel injection metering systems are very complicated mechanically and it can be a crushing blow financially if the metering system requires replacement.

The exhaust system comes in for a very careful examination and anyone who flies in light airplanes should be thankful for that. Virtually all single-engine airplanes merely direct airflow over part of the exhaust pipe to heat the cabin. Any cracks in that pipe will pump deadly carbon monoxide directly into the cabin with predictably disastrous results.

The metal alloy used in aircraft exhaust systems prevents them from rusting and corroding like automobile exhaust systems but the aircraft system can and does crack. All of the temperatures in an air-cooled airplane engine, including exhaust gas temperatures, are higher than those in a conventional automobile water-cooled engine. That extra heat means the metal in the exhaust system must expand and contract over a greater range and that can lead to cracks. Vibration also works to break up the exhaust system. The extra heat and the vibration combine to make an exhaust system crack one of the more common problems found during an annual inspection.

Fortunately, many exhaust pipe cracks can be welded satisfactorily, saving a significant amount of money compared with the cost of a new pipe. But welding must usually be done by a welding shop suited to handle the types of metals used in an aircraft exhaust system and that often means a delay in getting your airplane out of the shop.

Exhaust system cracks or blown exhaust gaskets will usually reveal themselves by leaving a grayish stain of powder on the pipe around the leak. But to see all of the pipe, heater muffs and protective covers must be removed and that is one more reason an annual inspection costs so much.

Engine oil will be drained and the filter changed. The oil filter and oil screen will be carefully examined for any metal

The flange on the left of this Piper Aztec exhaust stack is cracked badly and nearly broken off. It probably can be repaired by welding but the crack has already ruined the engine cylinder by allowing it to operate with reduced back pressure. This break is easy to spot but most are not nearly so obvious.

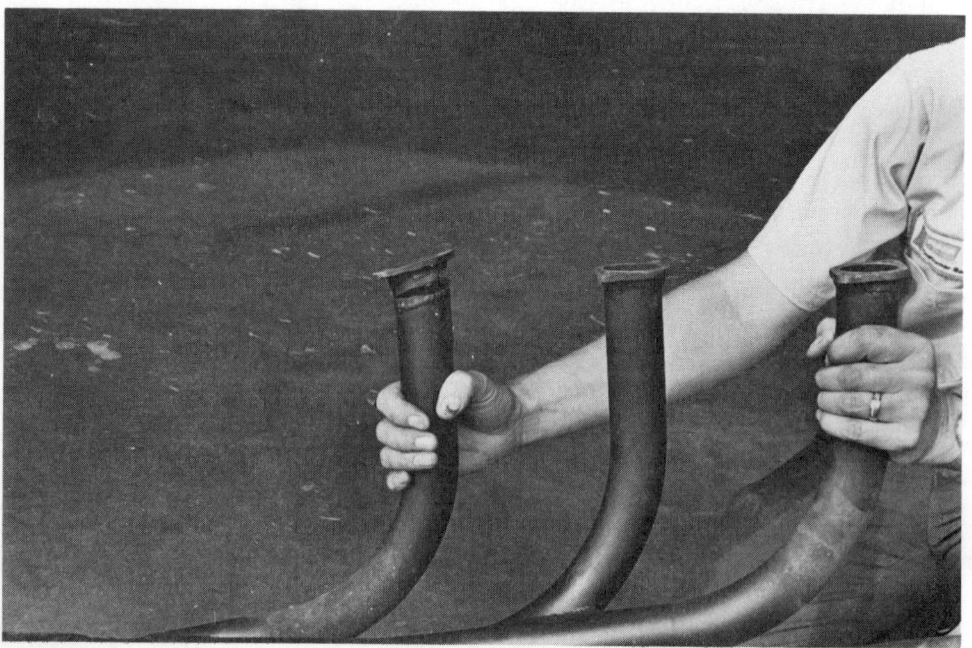

chips that may have broken off somewhere inside the engine and have been picked up in the oil sump. Most good mechanics will also have some type of screen over the can engine oil is drained into so any metal chips that may have been in the oil itself can be easily located. Highly sophisticated chemical analysis of engine oil is available to determine engine wear patterns and you may wish to have an analysis performed on your engine oil at annual inspection time. I'll have more on the potential benefits of oil analysis in the final chapter on safe and saving operating techniques.

At some point, usually early in the inspection of the engine, a solvent and high pressure air gun will be used to wash the entire engine and its compartment. A clean surface is essential for the inspector to detect cracks, leaks, or other problems with the engine and its systems. Once the engine has been reassembled it will be run up without the cowling and again visually inspected for oil or fuel leaks.

A clean engine is not only nice to own and nice to work on,

Engine wash down with high pressure air gun and solvent is an important part of any inspection. The solvent blasts loose any dirt and crud on the engine to permit a good visual inspection and also makes it possible to spot oil leaks if they appear after the engine work is finished.

it is a safety factor. A thick coating of grease and grime on a hot engine is a fire hazard. Even worse, it is impossible during preflight inspection to see if any oil or fuel leaks have developed.

A thorough examination of the propeller will be part of any annual inspection. Fixed pitch props are rather simple to inspect but a controllable pitch prop will require more checking.

The most important part of any propeller inspection is examination of the blades for nicks. Nicks can be the start of a crack in the blade and a crack can lead to blade separation in flight. If the tip breaks off a blade in flight, the engine is often ripped from its mounts by the severe vibration caused by extreme imbalance of the prop. If the engine falls off, the airplane will be unable even to glide to a landing and disaster can be the only result. Don't take prop nicks lightly because they can kill you.

Small prop nicks can be filed out by a qualified mechanic. The goal is to smooth the nick, deterring the start of a crack. Also, an equivalent amount of metal must be filed from the same position on the other blade or blades to keep the prop in balance. Large prop nicks will require the prop to be returned to a certified prop shop for dressing. If the nick is very near the end of the blade, the blades may be clipped down and the prop

A small nick on this prop blade has been repaired by using a file and fine grit sandpaper to smooth the surface. If a large amount of metal is removed from a blade during nick repair, a similar amount must be removed from the other blade to maintain balance.

rebalanced. If the nick is simply too deep, the prop shop must discard that blade entirely.

Controllable pitch props have bushings and oil pressure seals that can wear and must be examined during annual inspection. Excessive play in the blades or oil leaking from the prop hub are signs that a prop needs overhaul. Feathering props on twin-engine aircraft use gas under pressure in the prop hub dome to feather the prop blades. This gas pressure is checked during annual inspection as well.

A prop should also be checked for track accuracy. To perform this simple check the inspector will place some fixed object near a blade tip and then rotate the other blade or blades around to see how closely they align with the fixed object. This track test reveals any fore or aft bend in the blades.

Tires, wheels, and brakes will all receive detailed attention during an annual inspection. Tires will be checked visually and the inspector will not only try to determine if they are presently up to standard but if they will serve for any extended length of time. If a tire is still sound but near the end of its wear life, most authorized inspectors are going to want a new tire mounted before signing off the aircraft.

All wheels will be removed and the wheel bearings will be cleaned and packed with grease. Greasing the bearings is important in protecting bearing life but it is also important to get a good close look at the axle to be certain no cracks have developed which could let you down hard on landing.

Brakes can be a constant source of maintenance problems, especially if your airplane is tied down in thick grass and flies little. The grass will hold moisture against the brake disks, creating heavy rust on the steel disks. The first time you move the airplane and apply the brakes the brake pads will scrape away rust on the disks but will also scrape away part of the brake pads themselves. If the rust grows too thick on the brake disk it will pit the metal and those rough pits will accelerate pad wear even after the rust has been cleaned off. An airplane sitting in a damp tie-down ruins its brakes almost as quickly as an airplane that flies a great deal. There is nothing you can do to prevent brake disk rust except fly the airplane frequently and try to stay out of grass tie-downs.

This mechanic is holding a rusted and pitted brake disk which has been removed from the wheel. The rough surface of this disk would quickly wear brake pads, leading to a brake failure on landing. The best way to prevent brake disk rust and pitting is to keep your airplane wheels out of standing water or wet grass and to fly the airplane often so rust is polished away by the brake pads before it can pit the disk metal.

Hydraulic fluid leaks are another common brake problem. Most leaks occur around caliper seals and are not extremely difficult to repair if the leaks are spotted early. Big problems with brake calipers come when small leaks go unnoticed and the leaking fluid attracts dirt, sand, and other crud from the runway and taxiway. This dirt can work into the caliper mechanism and score the moving parts; in extreme cases dirt can actually freeze up the caliper mechanism. If either of these two problems exist, the caliper will probably have to be rebuilt, which means honing out the bore and replacing some parts. If caliper cylinder scoring is deep or if the entire mechanism is badly frozen, the only solution may be a new brake caliper, and that is expensive.

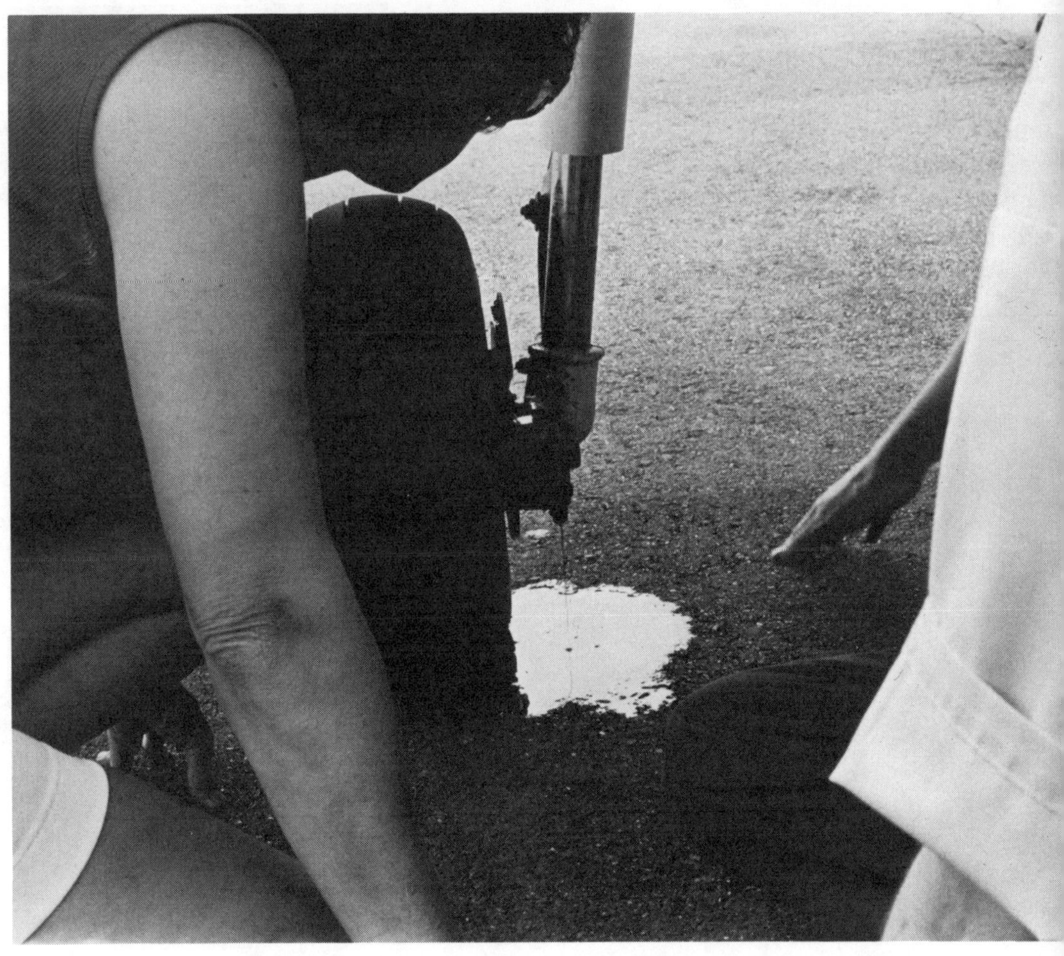

The brake piston O-ring has given way on this Cherokee brake leaving the airplane owners to stare at a puddle of hydraulic fluid leaking out on the ramp. A rusted disk wore away new brake pads allowing the piston to extend too far and the O-ring failed.

Every annual inspection should include a "lube job." With all the airframe inspection plates removed, good mechanics will take the opportunity to lubricate control cable mechanisms, bell cranks, hinges, pushrods, and just about any other operating mechanism on the airframe.

The first and final steps of an annual inspection are an engine run-up. The mechanic or authorized inspector will look for

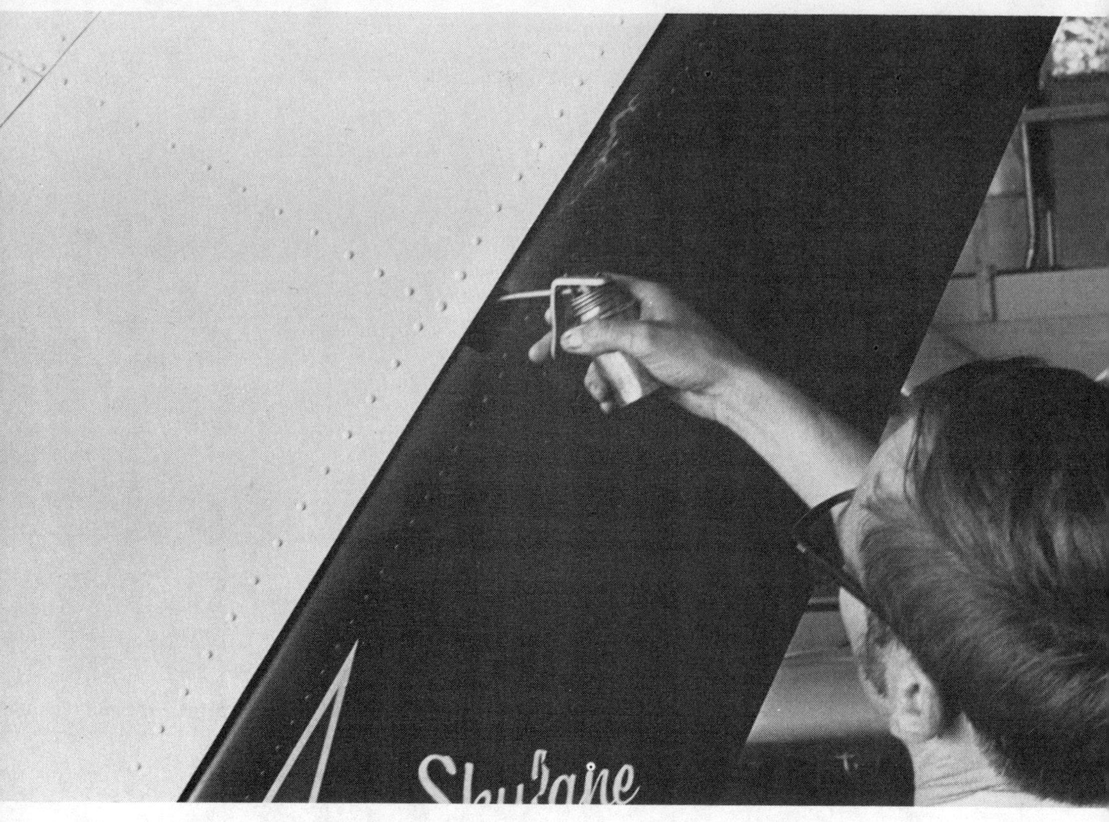

A few drops of oil from a squirt can should be applied to all control hinges during an annual inspection. Most mechanics will apply lubrication as they inspect so the entire job is completed in one trip around the airplane.

acceptable performance from the engine and all systems during the first run-up and again in the final check. Some authorized inspectors who are also qualified pilots may want to fly the airplane or fly with you in the airplane to observe performance of all systems in actual flight.

As you can see, the annual inspection is exhaustive and therefore expensive. The annual is designed to uncover problems early and a short series of even minor problems will quickly add up to a large shop bill. How to plan for the cost of an annual and what kind of cost estimate to expect for an annual will be covered in the chapter dealing with shop selection.

A 100-hour inspection is required for all airplanes used for hire. That means any airplane that is rented to others or used to carry passengers or freight for pay must be inspected every 100 hours of operation.

The 100-hour inspection is much the same as an annual in FAA eyes in that it calls for a "complete inspection of the aircraft, engine and all systems." However, the 100-hour can be completed by an A&P without approval of an IA. Even though the FAA indicates the 100-hour inspection is every bit as thorough as an annual, its importance is somewhat diminished because a mechanic of lesser experience and qualification can approve the inspection.

For the typical light airplane owner the 100-hour inspection will not be required. Most of us will never operate our airplanes for hire. Should we choose to split direct expenses for a trip with friends, the FAA does not view that as a commercial flight so no commercial pilot certificate or current 100-hour inspection is required. In fact, most private airplane owners are not going to operate their machines a great deal more than 100 hours in a calendar year in any case.

But if you are one of those rare individuals who flies several hundred hours a year you should consider 100-hour inspections even though they may not be required. A friend of mine flies 400 or more hours a year regularly, all on personal business. Even though his airplane requires only an annual inspection he sends it to the shop each 100 hours for a 100-hour inspection on the engine only.

A 100-hour on the engine would include all of the inspection and tune-up type work we covered for an annual. Engines are the largest single source of maintenance problems in light airplanes and my friend's reasoning is that 100-hour checks on the engine will spot problems early, saving money and increasing safety.

There is no general agreement among mechanics or aircraft manufacturers that 100-hour inspections are necessary if required maintenance, such as oil changes, is performed on schedule. However, the more often an airplane is inspected the better your chances of discovering problems early before the problem can become a safety hazard or add to repair bills.

There is a way to avoid annuals and 100-hour inspections

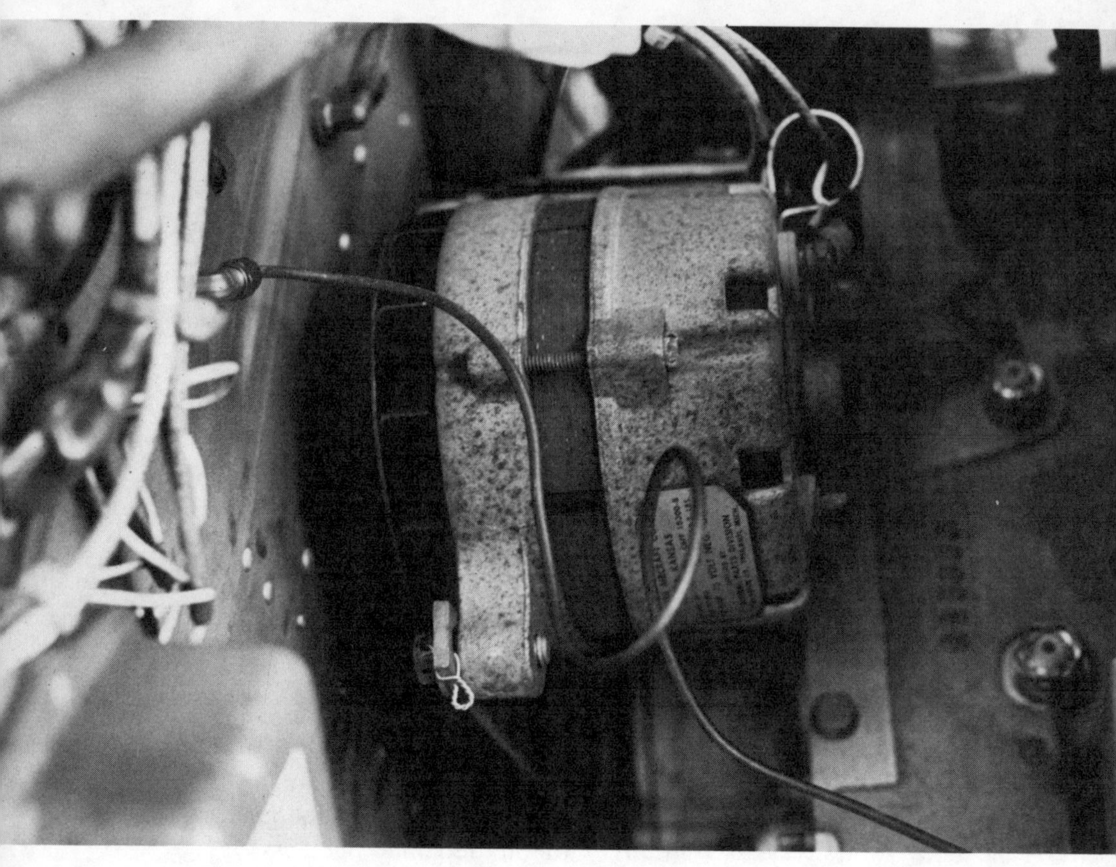

If you fly several hundred hours a year, 100-hour inspections of your engine may be valuable to spot problems such as worn alternator drive belts. It is a simple task to replace an alternator belt, but if it breaks in flight, especially during a night flight under IFR, you could be in for real problems.

completely and that is through a series of small inspections called "progressive inspections." Progressive inspections are used by most fleet operators such as airlines, charter fleets, and major instruction facilities. The primary advantage of progressive inspections is that an airplane spends less time in the shop on each visit and therefore less time out of service.

To be inspected under the progressive scheme, an aircraft is divided into sections and each section is inspected at a separate time. These inspections are called events and when all events are completed the aircraft has gone through an entire cycle. One cycle must be completed in each year.

Progressive maintenance can only be done with the direct approval of the FAA. Each aircraft type must have an approved cycle of events, which is determined by negotiating with the FAA. The exact events and cycle approved for one operator may not apply to another. Progressive inspection is great for fleet operators who have mechanics on staff but is not usually helpful to the private airplane owner.

Major flight schools find progressive inspections beneficial because mechanics working the night shift can complete an event and return the airplane to the flight line the following day. To perform a complete 100-hour inspection or annual would require a few days of downtime when the airplane would not be out flying students. The same is true of large corporate flight departments, which complete inspection events between trips without removing the airplane from service for more than a few hours.

I only know of one private airplane owner who used progressive inspections and in that case it didn't work out. This owner had a mechanic friend who could complete a progressive inspection event in an evening after finishing his normal workday. In this way the mechanic could keep the airplane in service without missing work at his regular job. But after a short period the number of events in the cycle became more bothersome than a normal annual inspection and the owner abandoned the progressive scheme.

If you fly a large number of hours each year or leaseback your airplane to an FBO who rents it out for a significant number of hours a year, progressive inspection may work for you. Oil changes come around every 50 hours on most airplanes and in a 500-hour year that is ten trips to the shop for oil changes. Those ten trips may be used for inspection events and to avoid the longer downtime needed for 100-hour or annual inspections. But most likely you will find the few days of downtime required for normal inspections less trouble than having your airplane approved for progressive inspections.

Airplane owners who fly IFR face additional required inspections of the aircraft static system, transponder, and VOR receivers. The VOR accuracy test is the easiest and may be performed by the pilot and is required every thirty days. The altimeter and static system must be inspected every two years by an approved shop. Also, the transponder must be checked by a certified radio shop every two years.

The VOR accuracy test used to be required every ten days or 10 flight hours but current radios are so much more reliable and accurate than earlier sets the FAA extended the time period to thirty days with no flight hour limit.

Many large airports have a VOT, which is a VOR test signal. By tuning to the appropriate frequency, which is published on IFR airport approach charts, this VOT test signal can be received on the ground at the airport. With the omni bearing selector (OBS) set at 360 degrees the VOT signal should cause the needle to center and the TO-FROM flag to indicate TO. If the needle centers with the OBS set within 4 degrees of 360, your VOR passes the accuracy test for thirty days.

Other airports that have no VOT but do have a VOR on the airport or nearby may have a designated ground checkpoint. At that specific point on the airport, which is published on the chart and usually marked with a sign on the taxiway or run-up pad, your VOR needle should center when set within plus or minus 4 degrees of the published radial.

An even easier way to meet the VOR test requirement when you have dual VOR receivers, which virtually everyone does to fly IFR, is to tune both receivers to the appropriate station while flying on a published airway. The two receivers should agree within 4 degrees to pass the check.

Finally, the AIM contains certain geographical landmarks you may fly over to test VOR accuracy. When over these points your VOR receiver must be within plus or minus 6 degrees of the published radial to satisfy the test requirement.

Approved avionics repair stations can also test VOR accuracy but must comply with a more complicated set of procedures using signal generators and other test equipment. However, even this complicated test performed by a shop is not good for more than the thirty days you get by checking the VOR receivers yourself. The FAA also says we must record the date and place where this VOR check was performed in a permanent record but that record keeping is probably the most ignored inspection in aviation. I am not saying you should ignore the VOR test requirement if you fly IFR because it is so simple to tune both receivers to the same station on an airway and check for accuracy but the record keeping need not be anything more exotic than writing the test date down on a piece of paper you keep.

Most shops will have the necessary equipment to test an aircraft static pressure system for leaks but altimeter check and calibration can be performed only by an approved repair station. The altimeter must be tested over a broad range both for accuracy and hysteresis. Hysteresis is lag in an altimeter, which may be caused by friction in the instrument gears or loss of resilience in the aneroid.

Obviously, it is an excellent idea to check the only instrument that determines altitude in light airplanes but the system is not foolproof. I departed on a night trip just after my altimeter had been exchanged for a newly inspected instrument which satisfied the two-year test requirement. This newly certified altimeter had a leak in the aneroid, which is the pressure sensing part of an altimeter, causing it to present erroneous altitude information. After a 500-mile IFR flight I nearly flew into the ground because the altimeter was indicating 1,400 feet more altitude than I actually had. In this case the old altimeter was working just fine and had been replaced by one that nearly led me to a nasty end. Sometimes inspections create problems rather than detect them.

A static system test must be performed any time the static system is disturbed or at least every two years. If the altimeter, airspeed indicator, or rate of climb indicator are disconnected from the static system or any other fittings are uncoupled, the system must be rechecked before flight under IFR. The check merely consists of pumping air pressure from the static system and observing the rate at which pressure leaks back in. However, this process requires special equipment and a special authorization for the shop. The static system test and altimeter test are two separate procedures and shops that have the authorization to check static systems may not have approval to test altimeters. In those cases the instrument will be sent to a certified instrument shop or may be exchanged for an altimeter that has been tested. The exchange program puts an altimeter back in the panel quickly but many owners want to have their altimeter tested and returned, not replaced by some other instrument. Either way should in theory work fine but with your altimeter you know more about the instrument and its past history.

The two-year transponder test is usually a simple procedure that takes minutes at an approved radio shop. A ramp tester which simulates a radar signal is used to interrogate the transponder and check its reply. This device is called a ramp tester because the transponder stays in the panel and the test signal comes in through the normal antenna. This check will test the transponder to see that it replies on the proper code and if you have an incoder that reports aircraft altitude on Mode C, that function will also be tested.

One of the least known required inspections deals with breathing oxygen bottles which fall under Department of Transportation (DOT) regulation. More and more turbocharged airplanes are entering the fleet so oxygen systems are now quite common and inspection will be required.

Aviation oxygen tanks are divided into two groups—lightweight and standard. Lightweight tanks must be checked every three years while standard tanks require examination only every five years.

The actual tank test consists of pumping 166 per cent of the tank's rated pressure into the bottle to see if it holds. If the tank explodes or expands beyond limits, it flunks the test. Of course, this test can only be performed by a shop with the safety facilities to contain an explosive failure which could be disastrous. Oxygen tanks often are rated at as much as 2,000 pounds per square inch with 1,850 psi common in aviation. Those pressures demand a great deal of integrity.

A standard weight oxygen tank, which can be identified by an ICC or DOT number, has no life limit so long as it continues to pass its pressure test every five years. Lightweight tanks must be discarded after fifteen years of service or after 4,380 pressurizations even if the tank is up to standard in its three-year test. It is unlikely any oxygen bottle in a light airplane will ever be filled 4,380 times but the fifteen-year life limit is certainly a factor to be aware of and plan for in a used airplane.

One of the most important aspects of all of these required inspections we have discussed is record keeping. Maintenance record keeping is required and is a shared responsibility of the owner and maintenance personnel. Neatness and thoroughness are two necessities for good record keeping and those qualities are among the factors you should look for in selecting a shop, which is discussed in the following chapter.

2

How to Identify a Quality Maintenance Shop

We all want the same things from an airplane repair shop. We want fast service with no waiting for parts or special attention from an inspector. The work must be done perfectly to save our necks in the air and prevent those really annoying return visits to correct an old problem. And, perhaps most vital to many of us, the price must be right. We have to receive the best possible maintenance service for our dollar or we can't afford to keep our airplanes.

When we go shopping for a maintenance facility with all these factors in mind there is one area which cannot be compromised—quality of work. No matter the savings in downtime or money, shoddy work is never a bargain. Even if no safety hazard is involved, doing a job quickly and improperly merely means it will have to be done again and there is no way doing everything more than once adds up to a savings in time or money.

Because we cannot accept anything less than the highest quality workmanship from a shop, only cost and downtime remain as negotiable factors. Some of us may be able to afford downtime more than a tremendously high repair bill while others find the most expensive airplane of all is one sitting on the ground rather than up in the air earning its keep. Often there is a link between how much a repair job or inspection will cost and how quickly it must be completed. But I'll get to that equation later; the first task in selecting a shop is to find one capable of quality work.

Identifying a good shop is not as easy as asking the supervisor. Obviously, no shop manager is going to say his hangar turns out anything but the best quality work. Instead, we must know what to look for and what questions to ask before visiting a shop.

The first consideration may seem obvious but many airplane owners ignore this most basic fundamental in shop selection—pick a facility familiar with your type of airplane. All shops charge for repairs based on the number of hours mechanics and inspectors actually spend working on an airplane. If your airplane is the first of its type these people have seen, you will not only be paying them to work on the plane but will be supplementing their educations as they learn all about where everything is on that particular model.

Finding a shop familiar with your type of airplane is not as easy as going to the nearest dealer who sells your brand of airplane. That will probably work well if your airplane is fairly new and of a popular type, but new airplane owners will already have

This display of service award and factory school certificates clearly indicates this shop is qualified to work on Piper airplanes. Such service centers can often be the most economical because mechanics associated with a new airplane dealership will have a great deal of experience with that specific type and should know what problems to expect and how to fix them.

learned about their dealer's service through the warranty period. The dealer is a good place to start but a Cessna dealership knew nothing more about the 1946 Cessna 140 I used to own than a Beechcraft or Piper dealer would. The airplane had been out of production for more than twenty years and was older than most of the dealership's mechanics.

In my case I searched for a shop that had experience with airplanes of that period. People who could work on old Champs, Cubs, and Taylorcrafts would most likely be able to do a good job on my 140. Those light postwar airplanes all used similar construction and virtually all depended on the small Continental engine series for power. Most new airplane dealerships don't have the capability to perform fabric cover work and would have no idea where to start an inspection on an airplane that is virtually an antique.

For more recent models such as the Cherokee series from Piper and the 172 and 182 series from Cessna, the dealership should be a logical place to start shopping for maintenance because no giant changes have been made in those airplanes over the years. However, the many small improvements made in those long-produced lines mean a shop must be well informed and documented to know exactly what to look for in each specific model.

The Beechcraft Bonanza model 35 series is an unusual airplane in that it has been in continuous production since 1947. Size, weight, systems, engines, props, and just about everything else have changed between the original V-tail Bonanza built in 1947 and the present V35B model but Beech has kept a steady flow of parts and maintenance literature going to its dealerships and most Beech dealers should be able to perform good work on your Bonanza no matter what the year or model. It is this continuity of production and support that continues to make the Bonanza the best single-engine airplane for holding its value on the used airplane market.

If there are no dealers selling your type of airplane nearby, the job of shop selection will be a little more difficult. In that case the best place to start is by finding some other owner with an airplane like yours and asking which shop he uses. If that is not possible, you'll have to visit shops cold and do the detective work on your own.

So let's say you have located a shop that you believe will be familiar with your airplane. Before turning your airplane over to this facility you should visit the shop and have a little talk with the maintenance supervisor.

First, try to get a look in the hangar where work is performed. Cleanliness is the hallmark of all quality shops. Floors should be swept clean, equipment should be orderly, and any small shops off the main hangar where work on accessories such as carburetors or electrical components is done should be clean enough to hold a dinner party. Dirty or disorganized tools and equipment are a symptom of dirty and disorganized work. Drip pans should be under any engine that could leak oil or any component that may drip other fluids. Airplanes are very clean by automotive standards and good mechanics keep them that way.

While you are in the shop look at the other airplanes in for inspection and maintenance. Are there any of your type? Is the work progressing in a logical manner as far as you can tell? If you see airplanes in the corner with missing parts and a coating of dust try to find out why. Don't let your airplane become one of those forlorn machines up on jacks or without its cowling for months.

Generally the reason those airplanes spend time gathering dust in the shops is because nobody has come up with the necessary parts to fix them. Find out how this shop procures its parts. If it is a dealership operation, you should expect it to maintain a considerable inventory of spares for its own brand of airplanes. If it is a small dealership, its parts inventory may be limited but in that case it should have rapid access to parts from a nearby distributorship. Standard "wear-out" parts like spark plugs, tires, batteries, brake pads, and so on, should be on hand at every shop. That type of part is common to many different airplanes and there is no excuse for a shop not to have them ready.

Airframe parts are going to be the most likely source of delay on any airplane and can be a real disaster for out-of-production airplanes. For airplanes less than twenty years old or for those that are still in production although as a slightly different model designation, the original manufacturer is going to be the

A well-stocked parts department is vital to a good maintenance shop. If normal wear-out parts such as tires and oil filters are not on hand, your airplane will spend more time in the shop. Also, a parts department associated with a new airplane dealership should stock a reasonably complete supply of parts for that brand of airplane.

best source of replacement parts. Old airplanes are usually supported by one or more of the national aircraft parts distributors who have been granted a license by the original airplane manufacturer to make airframe parts. If you have an airplane that is no longer supported by its original manufacturer, you should obtain literature and catalogues from a distributor who is producing parts so you know what is available and what it should cost. This information will help you plan time and expense for something when it breaks rather than leaving it all as a big surprise when the airplane goes into the shop.

After your visual examination of the shop is completed, ask the supervisor how often your type of airplane comes into the shop. If it is infrequent, beware and look again if they have never worked on that type of plane. If the foreman says he sees a lot of Brand X airplanes like yours, ask what he thinks is wrong if you are bringing the airplane in for a specific repair or what he thinks will be discovered if the airplane is in for an inspection. If the supervisor has in fact worked on and inspected many airplanes of your type, he will be able to either make a rather thorough diagnosis of the problem or expected problems from memory. Most airplane maintenance problems fall into patterns and if a mechanic or inspector truly knows your type of airplane, he will know what those common failures are and can tell you what he thinks the mechanics will find when they get the airplane opened up.

Because most maintenance problems do in fact quickly fall into a pattern there is voluminous literature printed on those problems by the original airframe or engine manufacturer and the FAA. Most of this literature is in the form of service bulletins from the manufacturer detailing problems to look for and how to fix those problems to prevent recurrence. If a problem is a safety hazard, the FAA will make that service bulletin mandatory in the form of an Airworthiness Directive Notification (AD Note), which means the problem must be corrected in the manner and time period prescribed by the FAA. AD Notes will be covered in greater detail in a later chapter.

Every good shop will have a complete library of service literature covering the airplanes it services regularly. Nothing is more frustrating to an airplane owner than to have a mechanic spend hours trying to diagnose a problem only to learn that it is in fact a common problem and its identification and solution have been covered in a service bulletin from the airplane manufacturer. But if these service bulletins are not filed properly, mechanics won't be able to find them and that ends up costing you money. Be sure to look for a well-organized library and you may even ask to see the specific book that covers your airplane. If it isn't there, this may not be the shop for you.

Okay, the shop looks clean, all work is progressing in an orderly manner as far as you can tell, and the shop foreman knows your airplane inside and out with a complete library of service bulletins to call on. What next? Now comes the estimate.

Estimating the time and extent of any mechanical repair job is difficult but on a machine as complex as the light airplane it

Look for a complete and organized library of service literature covering your type of airplane. If the shop does not maintain current published repair bulletins, you will pay for mechanics to search around and call for information that should be on hand.

borders on the impossible. Consider an annual inspection. The FAA says the entire airplane must be inspected and any problems with the mechanical condition of that airplane that could affect safety of flight must be corrected. What if you drove your car to the garage and told the mechanic to fix anything he could find that needed fixing? Would you expect to get a detailed and accurate estimate? It's impossible.

Beware of any shop that gives absolute estimates for inspections because that simply is not possible. A good shop can provide an estimate of shop time for the inspection and will stick to that estimate but that includes only the removal of inspection plates and so on to examine the airplane and engine. If you get a quote of $500 for an inspection, for example, the shop has no way of knowing what it will find wrong, so that price covers only

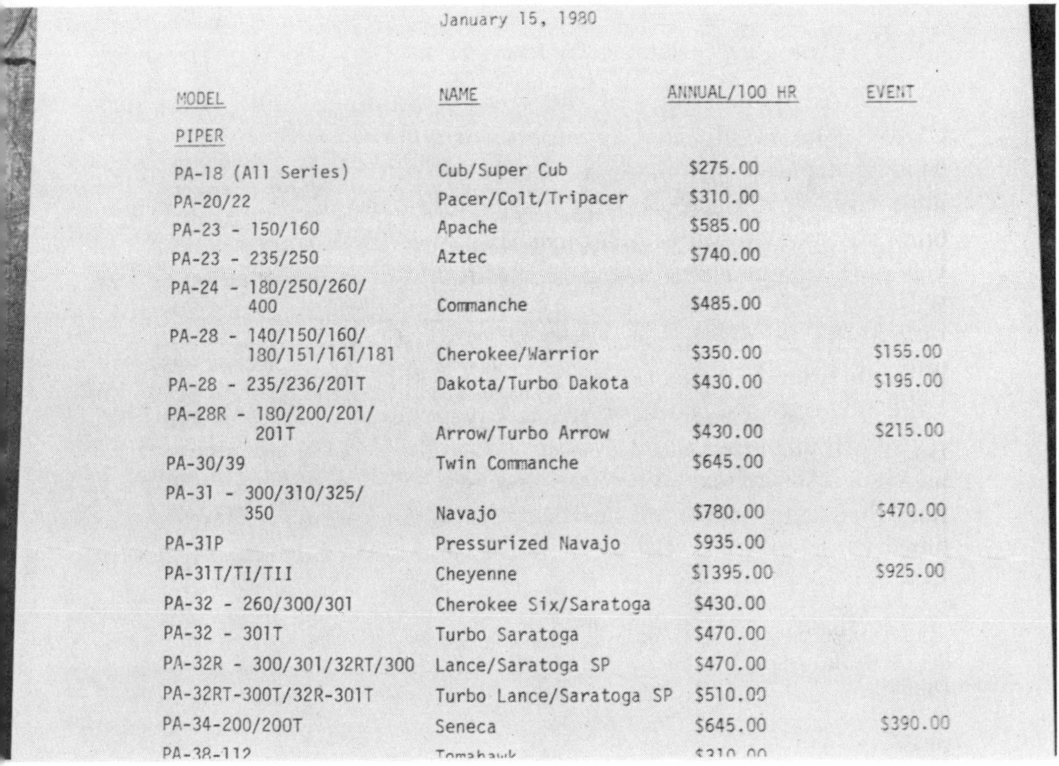

January 15, 1980

MODEL	NAME	ANNUAL/100 HR	EVENT
PIPER			
PA-18 (All Series)	Cub/Super Cub	$275.00	
PA-20/22	Pacer/Colt/Tripacer	$310.00	
PA-23 - 150/160	Apache	$585.00	
PA-23 - 235/250	Aztec	$740.00	
PA-24 - 180/250/260/ 400	Commanche	$485.00	
PA-28 - 140/150/160/ 180/151/161/181	Cherokee/Warrior	$350.00	$155.00
PA-28 - 235/236/201T	Dakota/Turbo Dakota	$430.00	$195.00
PA-28R - 180/200/201/ 201T	Arrow/Turbo Arrow	$430.00	$215.00
PA-30/39	Twin Commanche	$645.00	
PA-31 - 300/310/325/ 350	Navajo	$780.00	$470.00
PA-31P	Pressurized Navajo	$935.00	
PA-31T/TI/TII	Cheyenne	$1395.00	$925.00
PA-32 - 260/300/301	Cherokee Six/Saratoga	$430.00	
PA-32 - 301T	Turbo Saratoga	$470.00	
PA-32R - 300/301/32RT/300	Lance/Saratoga SP	$470.00	
PA-32RT-300T/32R-301T	Turbo Lance/Saratoga SP	$510.00	
PA-34-200/200T	Seneca	$645.00	$390.00
PA-38-112	Tomahawk	$310.00	

Many shops post their rates for inspections but this fee covers only the inspection and normal work during an inspection such as an oil change. Any defect found during the inspection will be an additional cost and there is no way a shop can predict what an inspection will uncover.

the inspection—the IA looking at your airplane and all of the other tests we talked about in the first chapter.

Good shops will tell you an inspection is going to cost you a flat fee plus the cost of correcting any discrepancies. Discrepancies is the word for something wrong, something that can't pass inspection. After initial inspection the shop supervisor will call you with a list of discrepancies and at that time will be able to provide a rather accurate estimate of what it will cost to get your airplane through the annual or whatever inspection is underway.

Most shop supervisors will be able to spot some discrepancies across the ramp. Worn tires, bad brakes, large prop nicks, and that type of problem can be identified early and taken into the cost accounting. But most problems will be hidden until the airplane is opened up and the engine examined and tested for compression. Again, a shop supervisor who is familiar with your type of airplane can make good guesses as to what will be wrong with your airplane based on his experience and on the service bulletins from the manufacturer. But those will only be guesses and nothing on which to base an estimate of your financial well-being.

If the same inspector has been working on your airplane through several inspections, he will be able to provide an even more accurate estimate of overall inspection costs. Most problems with airplanes don't pop up overnight and the inspector will have seen wear here and there and will know what needs attention this time around. For that reason and many others, it is worthwhile to stick with a shop that has been performing good

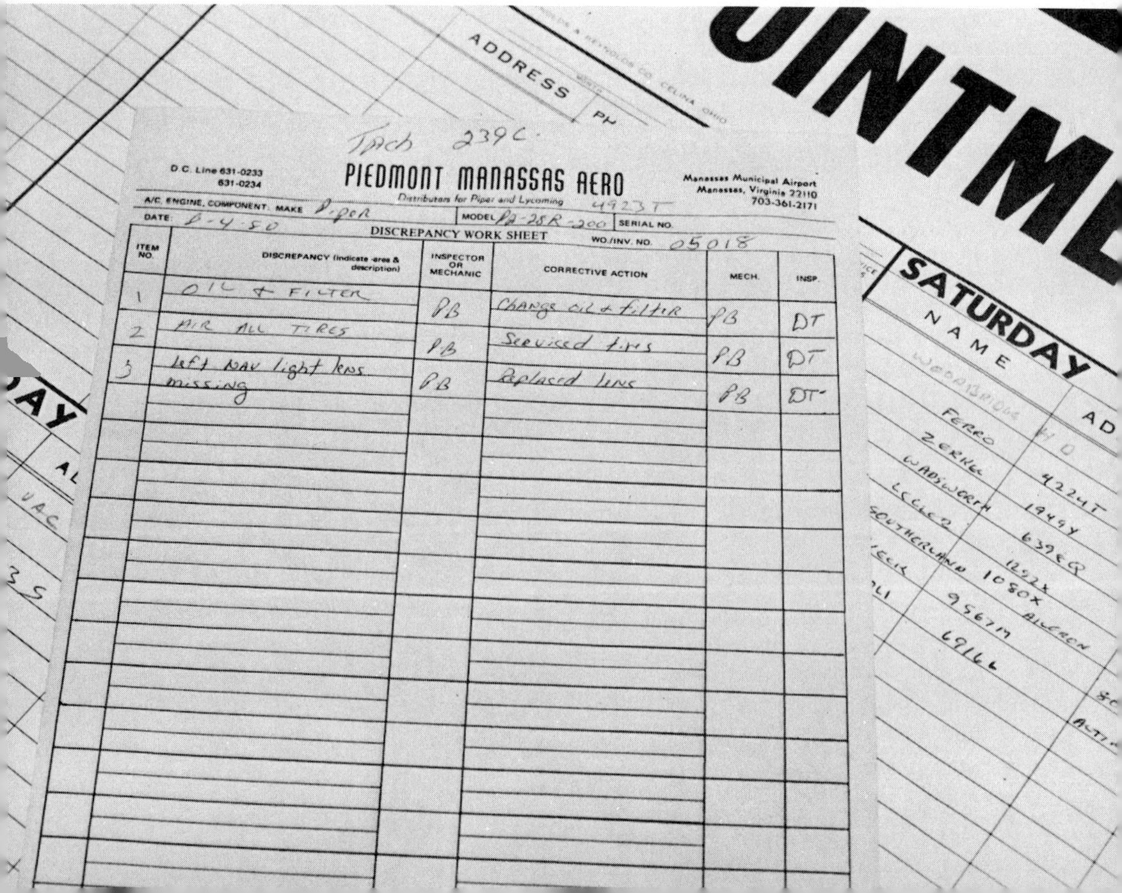

During an inspection the shop will fill out a discrepancy sheet listing all problems the inspection has uncovered. The FARs require all shops to present an owner with such a list and then it is the owner's decision where to have the discrepancies corrected. Once all discrepancies are identified any good shop should be able to give you an accurate estimate of repair costs.

work on an airplane even though it may not be the most convenient shop for you.

If this is your first time through an inspection since buying a used airplane, don't even consider what the former owner told you about last year's annual. It's too late to do anything now, you own the airplane. If last year's annual was cheap, it either means the airplane is in excellent condition and may breeze through inspection again or it may mean a poor shop signed off an airplane in marginal condition and it will need major work to pass inspection this time around. A very expensive annual doesn't buy you anything more than a year's worth of legal flying at best so don't think every big inspection bill is followed by a few years of low cost. It doesn't always work that way. At annual time all you can do is locate the best possible shop with knowledgeable mechanics using a complete library and parts stock and hope everything is well inside your airplane. Guessing what will be wrong at annual inspection time is virtually impossible and the surprises we find every year are one of the largest frustrations of light airplane ownership.

3

Maintenance Records:

What's Required and How to Keep Them

There is an old saw in aviation that no airplane is legal to fly until the weight of required paperwork equals the gross weight of the airplane. It takes nearly as much paper to keep an airplane flying as it does fuel and a large percentage of that pulp load deals with maintenance records.

As usual, the FAA spreads responsibility around with the airplane owner and operator, the last guy in line, to make certain aircraft paperwork meets the FARs. Mechanics and other maintenance service personnel are required to make entries in aircraft records in a specific manner but the bottom line responsibility for making certain everything is recorded as required is on the airplane owner or operator.

The need for maintenance records is clear. As we discussed in the first chapter, most service performed on an aircraft is of a scheduled or periodic nature. Without records to indicate when this work is due to be performed, regular inspections and routine maintenance would be impossible. Civil aviation authorities in this country have traditionally certificated airplanes under the fail-safe design concept. That is, U.S. approved airplanes are subject to testing with some parts failed and the remainder carrying the airframe load. Many other nations approve airplane designs under a life limited concept where that design is tested and approved for a specific amount of time in service before critical parts of possibly even the entire airplane must be replaced.

The foundation of the U.S. fail-safe scheme of design certification is regular inspection and testing of the airplane in service. That is why the FAA is so strict about regular annuals or 100-hours or the many other required inspections we discussed in the first chapter. In order to determine when these inspections are due, the owner or operator must record time in service and it is that owner or operator's responsibility to bring the airplane to maintenance personnel when scheduled inspections or service are required.

In general most mechanics and pilots refer to maintenance records as the airplane logbooks because this is the traditional way of keeping maintenance records. Logbooks trace their roots to the earliest days of flying when there were no recording tachometers or hour meters to keep tabs on flight time, so each flight was recorded in an aircraft log. These old airplane logs are much like a pilot's personal logbook with spaces to record where

Some manufacturers now offer loose-leaf maintenance records in addition to the conventional engine and airframe maintenance logs. The advantage of the loose-leaf record book is that pages can be added or discarded if they are no longer necessary. For example, the actual logbooks can be spared the clutter of entries for routine service such as oil changes.

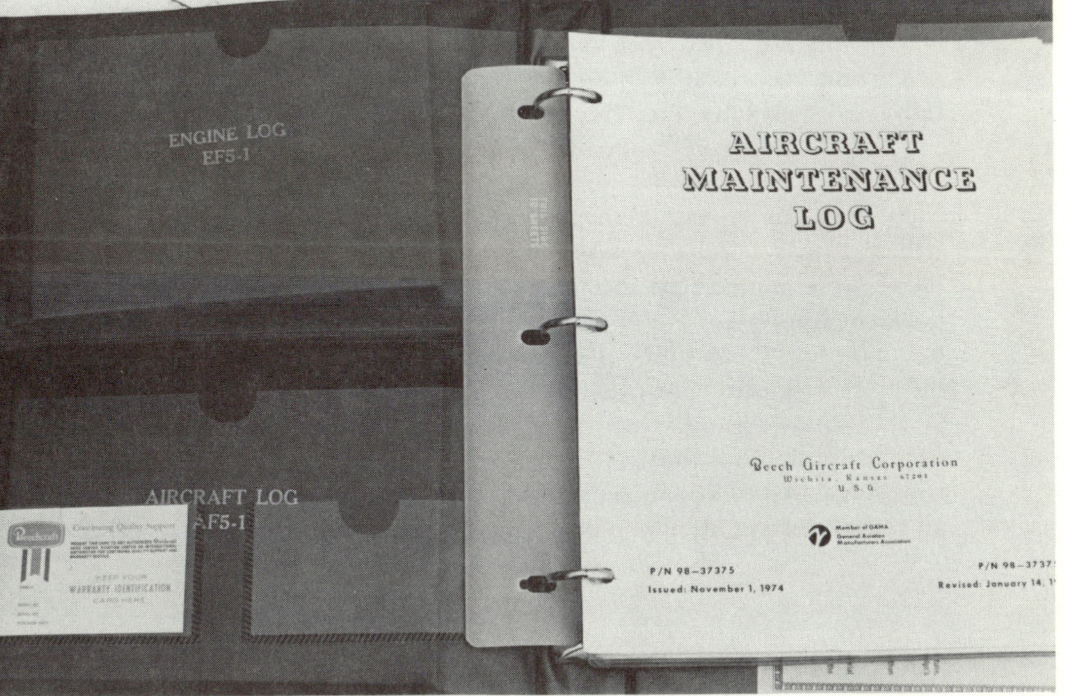

the flight departed and arrived, time en route, day or night conditions, and other details.

The old 1946 Cessna 140 I used to own had logbooks kept for the first twenty years of its life before an hour meter was installed to take over the task. However, when the mechanic who installed the hour meter transferred total time from the logs into a new style maintenance log he made a mathematical error and added 200 too many hours to the airplane's total time. In some ways it is sad to see the old logbooks go because I found it extremely interesting to see who was flying my old airplane and where it had been thirty years ago. An airplane with complete and detailed records is always worth more than an airplane with large holes in its maintenance history. When I sold the old 140 I found those early records captivated prospects and helped a great deal to bring the inflated price I was asking.

Typically a modern airplane will have a logbook for the airframe plus a separate log for each engine and if the propellers are controllable pitch, there will be logs for each prop as well. We still call them logbooks but the only information recorded is maintenance service performed and time in service for each operation and in total.

For added flexibility, some manufacturers are moving away from the logbook format for maintenance records in favor of a loose-leaf binder. The FAA makes no requirement as to the format of maintenance records and in fact encourages owners to keep some records in a loose-leaf binder because not all information must be retained for the life of the airplane.

Totally separate record books are not required for airframe, engine, and prop but it is required that you keep specific data for each item. However, if an airplane leads a long service life, it will use up several engines and propellers so when engines or props are changed it is most convenient to have separate record books or binders.

The length of time specific records must be kept will vary but it can require careful study to determine which records may be thrown away and which must be retained. Light airplanes do not accumulate all that much paperwork by volume so I think it is best to have an organized method of record keeping and retain all records of maintenance performed. These records do not need

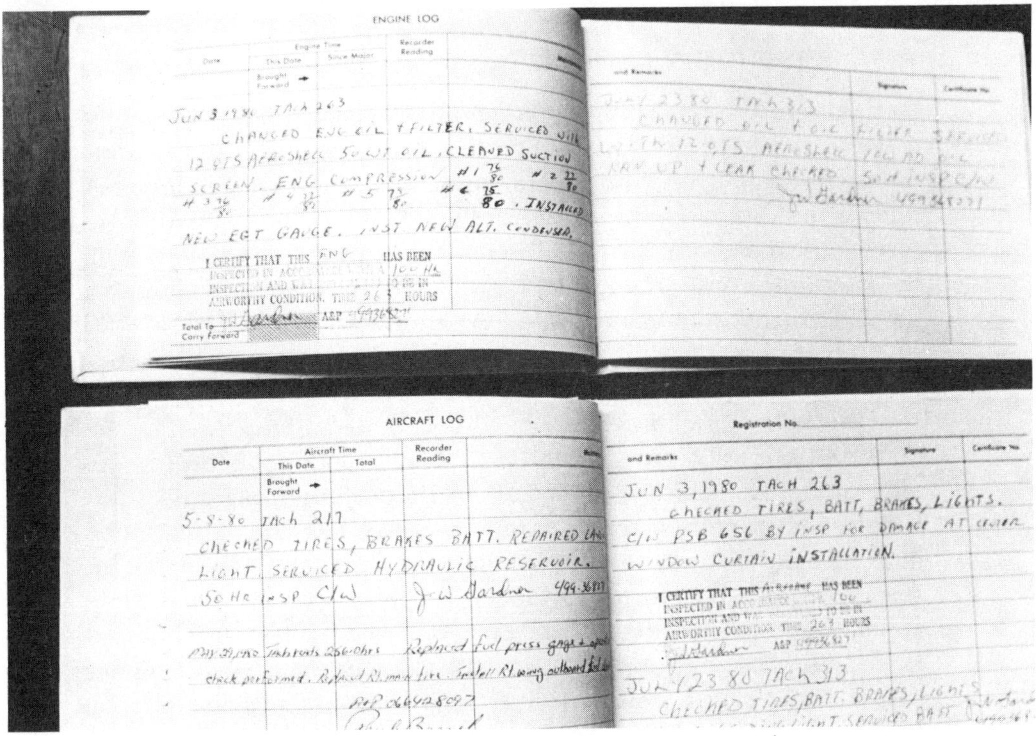

The engine and airframe logs pictured here show entries made for the same inspection. It is not required that engine and airframe records be kept in separate logbooks but that is best because an airframe will often have several different engines during its lifetime.

to be kept in the airplane as the only required maintenance record or notation that must be on board is proof that the airplane is not past its annual inspection date or 100-hour inspection if the plane is used for hire. Paper placards signed by an IA placed in the airplane and noting date and time of annual or 100-hour due will provide necessary proof of inspection.

The most basic and continuous information that must be kept in all maintenance records is time in service. For the airframe the records must always show a total time in service. Engines and propellers must show time in service but it is not always necessary to have total time in service because these components can be rebuilt and start over with zero time. However, that is not always the case and we will deal more with that subject in the chapter on major engine maintenance.

The most common way of keeping tabs on time in service is

by means of the recording tachometer or an hour meter, typically called a Hobbs meter for the firm that builds many of the meters. Simply having a recording tachometer or an hour meter does not relieve the owner of the responsibility of recording total time in service, or more specifically of being certain maintenance personnel keep total time in service recorded in the records. Each entry for an inspection or major repair or alteration must show a total time in service. That information can come from the tach or hour meter but must be recorded and retained in a written record.

Recording tachometers are also called engine hour meters and that more accurately describes their function—recording engine hours. A recording tach has no timekeeping capability but simply counts engine revolutions. The recorder will indicate one hour of engine time when the engine has turned enough revolutions to equal an hour of operation at normal cruise rpm setting. If the engine runs slower, the tach will record less than actual time passage, while if the engine is operated at a speed higher than normal cruise power, it will show more time passage than has actually taken place. Although the recording tach does not exactly reflect true time, it does reflect service time taken from the engine. An hour at high speed is harder on an engine than an hour at low speed and the recording tach accurately reflects that difference in wear and tear on the engine.

Hour meters are nothing more than little clocks that show in tenths or hundredths the length of time electrical power has been applied to the meter. Although these meters are quite accurate as timekeeping devices, large errors can be recorded if the hour meter is wired directly to the aircraft master switch. We have all left the master switch on at one time or another. When that happens an hour meter wired directly to the master will tick away until the battery goes completely dead and that can take many hours. These hours will show up on the hour meter as time in service when they are nothing more wearing than discharging a battery.

The best way to install an hour meter is with an oil pressure switch which is activated by oil pressure from the engine. In this way the hour meter records only those hours when the engine is operating and that is certainly a base line definition of time in service for both the airframe and engine. Wired to an oil pressure sensor switch, the hour meter will be a very accurate recorder of aircraft operation hours. If the meter is wired only to the master switch, I would believe the recording tach more than the hour meter for time in service.

Other than total time in service the only information that the FAA requires we keep is that detailing inspections and maintenance. The FAA is very careful to separate maintenance from preventive maintenance and there is no requirement to record preventive maintenance steps. Preventive maintenance is regular service such as oil changes, new tires, new paint, new interior, as well as other procedures that are required routinely. Obviously, oil changes and the like must be recorded somewhere so that you know when the next change is due, but I like to keep a separate record of preventive maintenance procedures so the permanent logbooks are not cluttered up with oil changes every 25 or 50 hours.

When it comes to major work on the airplane you will no doubt hear the term "337 form" from your shop. The 337 form is the typical way of recording major repair or alteration to the airframe, power plant, or propeller. The 337 is used to describe the work or equipment changes in detail and to show total time in service at that point and new weight and balance if any component weighing more than 1 pound has been added or removed. The 337 is an 8½ by 11-inch sheet of paper with little in the way of FAA supplied information to make it a "form." However, expect and demand that your shop type or print detailed descriptions of work performed on the 337 and be certain to retain the form in your records. Some new aircraft manuals or maintenance binders have special plastic holders for storing these bulky 337 forms along with the standard maintenance logs.

A 337 may not be required for every major repair if the certificated repair station has an approved form for recording its work. In this situation the work order form which details every step taken in the major repair may substitute for the 337. However, this procedure does not apply to major alterations and does not relieve the shop of the responsibility of recording basic information about the repair in the permanent maintenance record.

NOTICE

Weight and balance or operating limitation changes shall be entered in the appropriate aircraft record. An alteration must be compatible with all previous alterations to assure continued conformity with the applicable airworthiness requirements.

8. DESCRIPTION OF WORK ACCOMPLISHED *(If more space is required, attach additional sheets. Identify with aircraft nationality and registration mark and date work completed.)*

1. The purpose of this 337 is forthe installation of Whelen wing strobe lights.
2. Installed Whelen Model HDA-DF-14 power supply on fuselage floor at Station 115.0.
3. Installation made in accordance with STC SA 800EA/STC SA 615EA and AC 43.13-2 Chapter 2 following manufacturer's instructions.
4. Weight and balance data and equipment list revised.
5. All applicable F.A.R.'s complied with.

------------------------------------END------------------------------------

The reverse side of a 337 form contains a description of work performed, the really important part of any 337. All 337 forms become a part of permanent maintenance records and most mechanics will also keep copies on file for their own reference.

A major alteration sounds like a big project and you may think that applies only to cutting the wings off or some such drastic procedure. But the FAA says a major alteration is the installation or removal of equipment or accessories that weigh more than 1 pound. Installing a new radio is very common, but in FAA jargon that's a major alteration and you will get a 337 from the shop for a procedure as prosaic as that.

Another document that any shop must present to you as the airplane owner is a list of defects found during an annual inspection. This list does not become a part of the permanent records but it must be presented to the owner. If the defects are corrected as they must be for the aircraft to pass inspection, the shop will record steps taken to fix each problem. As the owner you have the option of taking the airplane to another shop to have these defects corrected and if an IA at that shop is satisfied that the airplane meets annual inspection requirements it can be

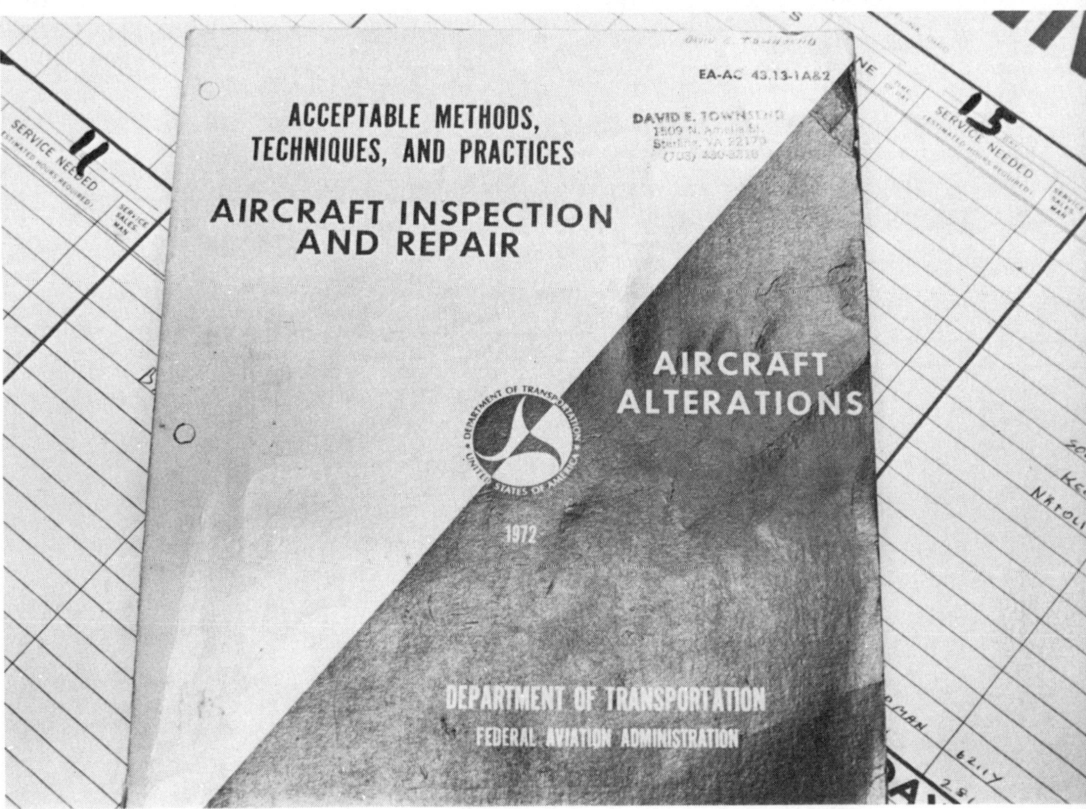

The FAA publishes a guide detailing acceptable methods and practices for aircraft inspections and alterations. Your shop should have this book and you may ask to see it if you are interested in how the work will be performed.

signed off and returned to service. There is *no* requirement that a shop provide the owner with a list of defects found in a 100-hour inspection although any good shop will present such a list.

If you are looking to buy a used airplane, it would be wise to spend more time searching through maintenance records than looking at the paint job and interior. Only in the maintenance records can you find a detailed history of the life your proposed new pride and joy has lived. New paint and interior can cover up a life of abuse and neglect but the maintenance records will tell the truth. If records are unavailable or incomplete, beware. Because the wording and information in aircraft and engine logs can be confusing, I think it would be worth a few bucks to have a reliable mechanic, preferably an IA, examine the records of any airplane you propose to buy. A mechanic familiar with the type of airplane you are considering will know what type of defect to be on guard for and can look at both the records and airplane to get a reasonable idea of what you can expect to go wrong in the near future.

After you buy the airplane or if you already own one, remember that it is your responsibility to see that every time it goes into the shop, maintenance personnel neatly and completely record the work performed. It is another one of those FAA double jeopardy situations where the mechanics are required to record entries of all work and inspections but we the pilots must make sure those entries have been made before we take off.

Preventive Maintenance an Owner-Pilot Can Legally Perform

Unreliable service, high prices, and a renewed feeling of independence in this country are leading to more and more do-it-yourself projects. The home improvement supply stores are booming. People from every social status are changing the oil in their own automobiles. And the FAA says if we as airplane owners and pilots have a mind to, there are many preventive maintenance jobs we can do ourselves.

The FAA is very careful to keep what it calls maintenance separated from what it calls preventive maintenance. Only properly licensed mechanics may perform maintenance but there are twenty-five specific preventive maintenance procedures any licensed pilot may perform on an airplane that pilot owns or operates. These procedures are detailed in Part 43 of the FARs.

As usual, the FAA has written the most restrictive possible meaning into its preventive maintenance regulations and there are two key concepts we must be aware of. First, a pilot is allowed to perform preventive maintenance only on an airplane that pilot owns or operates. That means if you have a pilot's license and are handy with tools and mechanical things you can do work on your own airplane, but you are not permitted under the FARs to work on a friend's airplane. To "operate" an airplane could mean that you lease it or are a member of a club that owns or rents the airplane on a fixed agreement that may be construed as a lease. In that case you could work on the airplane. The second catch the FAA has built into the preventive maintenance rules is a requirement that you have the necessary equipment, tools, and test apparatus and use acceptable methods, techniques, and practices as specified by the FAA or equipment manufacturer. That disclaimer can be found in FAR 43.13.

The bottom line of FAR 43 is that while an owner-pilot may perform some preventive maintenance tasks on his or her airplane many of the twenty-five specific preventive maintenance tasks will be impossible for the individual owner-pilot to perform because the required equipment would be far too expensive to buy for use on a single airplane. Because we can't as pilots work on airplanes owned by others, all equipment purchased for maintenance work can be used only for our airplane, making a cost-saving payback highly unlikely.

But don't give up on doing some preventive maintenance yourself because there are a few jobs that demand very little in the way of equipment or expertise and doing them yourself could save you some money. The place to start, however, is by examining the maintenance procedures we are permitted to perform. These procedures are listed in Appendix A of FAR 43.

Preventive maintenance. Work of the following type is preventive maintenance:

(1) Removal, installation, and repair of landing gear tires.

(2) Replacing elastic shock absorber cords on landing gear.

(3) Servicing landing gear shock struts by adding oil, air, or both.

(4) Servicing landing gear wheel bearings, such as cleaning and greasing.

(5) Replacing defective safety wiring or cotter keys.

(6) Lubrication not requiring disassembly other than removal of nonstructural items such as cover plates, cowlings, and fairings.

(7) Making simple fabric patches not requiring rib stitching or the removal of structural parts or control surfaces.

(8) Replenishing hydraulic fluid in the hydraulic reservoir.

(9) Refinishing decorative coating of fuselage, wings, tail group surfaces (excluding balanced control surfaces), fairings, cowling, landing gear, cabin or cockpit interior when removal or disassembly of any primary structure or operating system is not required.

(10) Applying preservative or protective material to components where no disassembly of any primary structure or operating system is involved and where such coating is not prohibited or is not contrary to good practices.

(11) Repairing upholstery and decorative furnishings of the cabin or cockpit interior when the repairing does not require disassembly of any primary structure or operating system or interfere with an operating system or affect primary structure of the aircraft.

(12) Making small simple repairs to fairings, nonstructural cover plates, cowlings, and small patches and reinforcements not changing the contour so as to interfere with proper airflow.

(13) Replacing side windows where that work does not interfere with the structure or any operating system such as controls, electrical equipment, etc.

(14) Replacing safety belts.

(15) Replacing seats or seat parts with replacement parts approved for the aircraft, not involving disassembly of any primary structure or operating system.

(16) Trouble shooting and repairing broken circuits in landing light wiring circuits.

(17) Replacing bulbs, reflectors, and lenses of position and landing lights.

(18) Replacing wheels and skis where no weight and balance computation is involved.

(19) Replacing any cowling not requiring removal of the propeller or disconnection of flight controls.

(20) Replacing or cleaning spark plugs and setting of spark plug gap clearance.

(21) Replacing any hose connection except hydraulic connections.

(22) Replacing prefabricated fuel lines.

(23) Cleaning fuel and oil strainers.

(24) Replacing batteries and checking fluid level and specific gravity.

(25) Removing and installing glider wings and tail surfaces that are specifically designed for quick removal and installation and when such removal and installation can be accomplished by the pilot.

Now that we know what procedures we may perform, let's go through the list and discuss each item and its problems versus possible cost savings.

Tire Changes

At first glance this sounds like a reasonably simple job. We have all changed tires from the time we had our first bicycle and it wasn't really that tough. But airplane tires and wheels are a different design from any most of us have ever encountered before. This procedure is full of problems for the amateur mechanic and the risks of damage to the airplane are very great.

The first problem, as we all know from our last flat tire, is to jack the machine up. There are no bumpers or handy frame members on an airplane to slide the trusty jack under. An airplane rests on three points rather than four so we can expect a change in its at-rest geometry to produce some unusual changes in its static stability, which is a complicated way of saying when you jack up one end or corner it can fall over on the nose, tail, or wing tip. But the greatest risk is that the jack can slip and punch a hole through the airframe.

Low wing airplanes have built-in jack points which are a reinforced area along the wing spar. These jack points are typically near the main landing gear strut on the lower surface of the wing. Jack points are just that, points. Miss the point by an inch and you will leave a hole in the wing skin. A friend of mine took his new Mooney to a dealer for an inspection and the mechanic, either in a hurry or just plain sloppy, put the jack under a drain hole instead of the nearby jack point hole and punched the jack right through the wing.

To jack up a high wing Cessna with spring landing gear struts requires a device that clamps onto the landing gear leg and provides a pad for the jack. Jacking up a spring landing gear

A special clamp has been fitted to the main gear strut of this Cessna 182, allowing the wheel to be jacked up using a normal shop floor jack. Without this special landing gear jack pad, jacking up the airplane would be risky if not impossible.

airplane after you have the special clamp is rather easy and not risky because even if the airplane falls off the jack the jack is low enough not to damage the airframe. Older high wing airplanes that do not have spring landing gear, such as the Piper Cub, can be jacked up by placing the jack under the main landing gear axle. Care must be taken that the jack does not slip in this situation because it will almost certainly punch a hole in the landing gear strut fabric cover and may damage the gear strut itself.

If you decide you have the equipment and want to raise your airplane on jacks, try to do the job inside a hangar because even a moderate breeze can easily blow an airplane off the best jacks. If it is not possible to get into a hangar, select a calm day and stay away from any operating aircraft because a prop blast could do as much damage as wind.

On any modern airplane, once the aircraft is safely raised on jacks, the do-it-yourself mechanic faces a gray area of FAR legality. The problem is that the FARs do not allow an owner-pilot to disassemble main landing gear brakes, but to remove the main wheel part of either Cleveland or Goodyear brakes, the two most common types, the main brakes must be partially disassembled.

It is not difficult to remove the outer caliper of a Cleveland brake so the wheel will slide off but it is not legal under the FARs. Goodyear brakes typically found on light airplanes have a floating disk which slides within the wheel to adjust for brake puck wear. These brakes are slightly more complicated than the Cleveland wheels but it would not be difficult to remove a

The brake disk and brake caliper are clearly visible in this photograph of a Cleveland wheel. It is impossible to remove the wheel without first removing the caliper because the disk is bolted to the wheel. FARs do not allow owner-pilots to disassemble brakes.

Goodyear brake and wheel if it were legal. I cannot, especially in view of the FAA's present hard line enforcement policy, recommend that you violate the FARs by disassembling any portion of the main wheel brakes.

Older airplanes such as the J-3 Piper Cub use an expanding-type brake which will not be involved with a wheel removal. If you have one of these older airplanes with the internal bladder-type brake, the wheel will slide off, leaving the brake intact and the procedure will be completely legal. To remain within the FARs, owners of airplanes with any other type of brake can remove only the nose wheel.

The next problem a prospective tire-changer faces is that an airplane wheel is a self-contained unit, not a wheel bolted to a hub as is the case with an automobile. When an airplane wheel comes off, the bearings and cones will come with it. Typically, a large nut with a cotter key holds the wheel to the axle. Removal of this nut allows the wheel and bearings to slide off.

Virtually all airplane wheels are two-part structures bolted together to hold the tire firmly between the wheel rims. To replace a tire the bolts are removed and the wheel split in half. However, and this is extremely critical, all air pressure must be released before the bolts holding the wheel together are removed. If the bolts are loosened with pressure still in the tire, the outer half of the wheel can become a projectile, capable of tearing off hands, arms, or worse.

Most aircraft tires have inner tubes and given the complexity of a tire change it is usually wise to replace the tube along with the tire. If the tire is still serviceable and only the tube is to be replaced, mark both the tire and wheel with a marker so the tire can be replaced on the wheel in the same position to retain proper balance.

When the wheel is reassembled care must be taken so the tube will not twist or pinch inside the tire. Many mechanics coat the tube and inside of the tire with talcum powder so the tube can more easily slide into proper alignment as air pressure is applied. To reinflate the tire it is best to use a clamp-on type of air hose fitting so you can clamp the fitting to the inner tube stem and stand clear as the tire inflates. Sometimes when the tire bead snaps into place it does so with such force that the wheel rim

With the retaining bolts removed, an airplane wheel splits into two pieces for a tire change. If air pressure is not released before the wheel bolts are removed or even loosened, the wheel halves could fly apart with enough force to cause very serious injury.

shatters or the bolts holding the wheel together break and the flying wheel rim could cause serious injury or even kill you. Many shops use a special cage to surround wheels during inflation to protect mechanics in case something fails.

When the wheel is ready to be replaced on the landing gear it should be checked for proper balance if either the tire or tube have been changed. Airplane tires are small in diameter compared with standard automobile tires, so they roll at much higher rpm, making balance even more critical than for a car wheel. Balancing requires special equipment either to static balance the wheel while it is at rest or dynamically balance it as it spins.

The bottom line on tire changes is that this procedure is best left to a qualified maintenance shop. There is the cost of the necessary equipment and the accompanying risk of jacking up the airplane; the gray legal area of brake disassembly on most airplanes; the danger of working with a split wheel under high air pressure, and finally the very real need to check wheel balance. Rather than tackling this job yourself, I recommend that during annual inspection when the wheels must be removed for examination, any tire that appears to be near the end of its life be replaced. The labor charge for tire replacement will be absorbed by the cost of the annual and you won't face a flat or worn-out tire during the next year.

Replacing Elastic Shock Absorbers

Elastic main landing gear shock absorbers are found on many of the fabric-covered light airplanes built just before and after World War II. These cords are commonly called bungee cords and they work quite well in actual service. The FARs say we as owner-pilots can replace these cords but I don't believe it is either wise or efficient to do so.

Bungee cords are really big rubber bands about ½ inch in diameter. These cords are not only capable of holding up the airplane on the ground but also absorb the shock of landing, so you can imagine the energy in these cords—and that is the problem.

Installed, the bungee wraps around two sliding links between the main landing gear strut and fuselage framework. The bungee is stretched tightly around the links to hold the airplane up at rest and stretches further to absorb landing shock. Like all elastic material, these cords eventually lose resilience and must be replaced.

To replace the bungees the slide links are removed from the airplane in a single unit and a new cord is stretched over these links. The super strength of these cords makes them dangerous to anyone not trained in proper procedures and not using equipment designed to protect the installer. If you get your finger pinched between the cord and sliding links, you could lose it. I just can't recommend that any owner-pilot tackle a bungee change without proper equipment, which is expensive and bulky.

Instead, try to find a shop where you can take your bungee link assembly for new cord installation. Once the cord is mounted on the sliding link assembly you can safely install the entire assembly in the airplane.

Don't assume that every time a main landing gear fails to re-

Opposite Page:
Top:
Bungee cords are usually found in older light airplanes such as a J-3 Cub or Aeronca Champ but they are also used in larger airplanes such as this Aero Commander. In this application the bungee cords are part of the landing gear retraction system and you can see how large and powerful these giant rubber bands really are.

Bottom:
The shock-absorbing bungee cords on this J-3 Cub are housed inside the wide areas of the landing gear struts. If you wish to replace bungee cords yourself, simply remove the entire bungee assembly and take it to a qualified shop. The powerful cords can be dangerous to install without proper equipment.

turn to normal upright position after a landing that the cords must be replaced. Lift the wing on the low landing gear side and the gear should snap back into place. If it fails to snap back tightly or the gear sags after you lower the wing, it's time for new bungee cords.

Servicing Air-oil Gear Struts

The air-oil, or oleo strut as it is commonly called, is the most common form of landing gear shock absorber and aircraft support system in use in light airplanes. Even the light Cessna singles which use a spring-type main landing gear have an oleo strut to support the nose wheel.

In many ways an oleo aircraft strut is much like the shock absorbers on an automobile. The main structure attached to the aircraft frame is in the form of a cylinder into which the lower portion slides. The cylinder is filled with oil that flows between the cylinder and piston through a small orifice. This oil flow acts as the primary shock absorber to cushion landing impact. A pocket of highly compressed air at the top of the cylinder forces a certain amount of oil back through the orifice and acts as a cushion for small shocks encountered during taxi and ground maneuvers. Air pressure is what keeps all of the oil from flowing through the orifice and flattening the strut to its stops.

The FARs say we can add both oil and air pressure to oleo

Opposite Page:
The amount of landing gear strut piston exposed here should tell you that the oleo strut on this Piper Arrow is properly inflated. If the strut is low on either oil or air pressure, little of the shiny strut piston will be visible.

struts but as is the case with most preventive maintenance procedures it is not that simple to accomplish. First, you must purchase the specific type of oil recommended by the airplane manufacturer and that means you'll probably end up buying a gallon when all you need is a pint. Second, you must have a source of high pressure air, which is normally supplied by a strut pump. A strut pump is a device that mechanically boosts normal air pressure from a shop compressor to the value necessary for servicing landing gear struts.

Another drawback to self-servicing of oleo struts is that many manufacturers recommend the use of nitrogen instead of air as the compressible gas. Nitrogen is inert and more stable than air and thus performs better in the oleo application. Air will work fine but nitrogen helps avoid any possible corrosion and abides by manufacturer's recommendations, which is what the FAA requires. Obviously, high pressure nitrogen is not something that is readily available to the do-it-yourself mechanic.

Should you decide to service your oleo struts because they appear low on inflation, consult your aircraft handbook for proper inflation value. This is usually given as a measurement of piston exposure when the airplane is at some standard empty weight. If, on examination of the oleo strut, there is no obvious sign of an oil leak there is a reasonable chance that the strut is merely low on gas pressure. To add pressure, locate the air valve fitting at the very top of the strut. On most low wing airplanes an access cover in the top of the wing skin directly over the main landing gear must be removed to reach the valve. The air valve is identical to those used on a tire for inflation and a tire-type air hose fitting will work. You may try applying the available air hose pressure you have on hand to the valve and see if the strut rises. If it does, add enough air to expose the recommended

Nitrogen from a large cylinder is being fed into the nose gear oleo strut on this Piper Archer. Nitrogen is superior to air for use in oleo struts because it is less impacted by changes in temperature.

amount of piston. If you have insufficient air pressure available, a strut pump will be required.

Adding oil to an oleo is more complex. The airplane must be jacked up off the ground and air released through the air valve much as you would deflate a tire. Then, following the prescribed procedure for your airplane, the air valve will be screwed out and the strut extended fully or to some other specified distance. Oil is added through the air valve opening and the strut is then fully depressed to force excess oil and any trapped air out of the air valve opening. After this procedure the strut is properly filled with oil. The airplane is lowered to the ground and the strut is inflated with air or nitrogen to its proper level.

While you may be able to service an oleo strut successfully

This mechanic is pointing to the air-oil filler point on the nose gear oleo strut of a Piper Archer. Air or nitrogen pressure is added through the valve, which is exactly like a tire air fill valve. Oil is added after pressure is released and the valve is screwed out.

using normally available air pressure, I believe this is a procedure best left to the professionals who have the necessary equipment and materials. However, we can all apply grease to the fittings and control link joints that are found on every oleo strut. By keeping these lubrication points well greased both the strut and the seals will be subject to less wear and that adds up to retention of proper oil-air inflation.

Servicing Wheel Bearings

Servicing wheel bearings is permitted under the FARs but involves wheel removal, jacking up of the airplane, and the legally gray area of partial brake disassembly we discussed in the section covering tire replacement. Servicing wheel bearings between annual inspections should not be required unless the airplane is parked in standing water or very thick grass, which can wash the grease out of the bearings and allow corrosion to set in. However, any time a wheel is removed for whatever reason, the bearings should be cleaned and packed with grease and that is a procedure we as owner-pilots can legally perform.

The first step in wheel bearing service is to check the bearings and cones for any sign of water. If water is found, the bearings should be completely cleaned in solvent so that new grease may be packed in, eliminating water and the corrosion it causes.

The split ring and grease seal have been removed, allowing the outer wheel bearing on this wheel to be removed. Most airplane wheels use roller bearings rather than ball bearings and the entire assembly must be packed with approved grease.

If the bearings are clean and free of moisture, packing with grease will be enough.

There are machines that use air pressure to force grease into bearings but the most common method of packing bearings is the old-fashioned stick your fingers in the grease can and push the grease into the bearing method. The airplane manufacturer will have recommended a specific type of grease to be used on the wheel bearings and to remain within the FARs that is the only grease you may use.

With all elements cleaned and greased it is time to reassemble the wheel and place it on the axle. Place the inner cone and bearing race in place and slide the wheel into place. Aircraft wheels always have some system of retaining the grease and keeping moisture out. This system may include large washers or rubber or felt seals, so be sure these items are in good condition and in the proper place.

After the outer bearing and cone are installed, the wheel retaining nut must be properly tightened. If the nut is too tight, the bearings will bind, too loose and the wheel will wobble. To set proper bearing tension, spin the wheel slowly as you tighten the retaining nut by hand. At some point the wheel will slow from friction as the bearings just start to bind. Back the nut off to

This single large nut holds the main landing gear wheel in place. Notice the cotter key barely visible on the left and right sides of the nut.

the next available cotter key hole alignment and secure the nut in place with a new cotter pin.

Replacing Safety Wire or Cotter Keys

To the uninitiated an airplane may appear to be held together with baling wire because there is so much fine wire wrapped around, especially on the engine. This wire is really safety wire that holds the nuts and bolts in place so those nuts and bolts can hold the airplane together, and the FARs allow owner-pilots to replace safety wire as necessary.

Unlike many preventive maintenance procedures we pilots are allowed to perform, replacing safety wire or cotter keys is not difficult and does not require a great deal of expensive equipment. On the other hand, safety wire doesn't need replacement often unless it has been cut away to remove the nut or bolt it has safetyed. However, if you have an older airplane, you may find corroded safety wire that needs replacement. Also, whenever you perform other preventive maintenance such as changing engine oil, the oil drain plug, oil filter, oil screen, and items critical to safe airplane operation will be secured by safety wire or cotter keys, which must be removed and replaced to complete the procedure.

Modern airplanes use less safety wire than airplanes of the World War II period, for example. Years ago the prevailing concept was that any nut or bolt used should be safetyed in some way but current studies have shown that tightening nuts and bolts to their proper torque value is sufficient in some applications. There will always be a need for safety wire, cotter keys, and friction nuts but none of these devices is a substitute for the correct torque setting of the nut or bolt. If the torque value is proper, there is little chance the nut can work loose. If the torque setting is not correct, the nut or bolt could fail even though safety wire or a cotter key keeps it from turning.

To replace safety wire you must first buy safety wire, which is a specific type of wire approved for aircraft use and available in various sizes according to the application. The wire is packaged in a small round container and is pulled out through the top

The screws holding this oil filler spout to the engine are safety-wired together to prevent them from working loose. Notice how the wire is twisted between the screws to add rigidity and also note that the tension of the wire pulls the screws tight, not loose.

of the container as needed, keeping the remainder of the wire neat and free of kinks inside the can.

Safety wire will usually be found on bolts where it is not possible to place a cotter key through a nut on the other end. Small holes through the bolt head receive the wire and often bolts will be safetyed together in a series with the wire twisted between each bolt head. Before removing the old wire, examine the old safety wire to see how it was done and what items were wired to what. Remember that the safety wire should always be wrapped to pull the bolt tighter. That means the wire should wrap around the bolt head in a clockwise fashion for right-hand threaded bolts, the most common type of thread in all applications.

To start a safety wiring job, cut more wire than you believe

Safety wire, like any other material used on airplanes, must be of a specific type approved for use. Safety wire comes in several thicknesses and is usually stored in round containers.

the job will require. Feed the wire through the first bolt or fitting to be safetyed and bring the two ends of wire together, much the way you would thread a sewing needle. Twist the wire together using approximately eight to ten turns per inch. The twist should be uniform in tension to add stability and rigidity to the wire and for a neat-looking job. There should be no excess wire between bolts or screws being safetyed and the wire should always remain firmly in place and not flap around where it could snag some component.

If the item is safetyed to a primary structure, the way oil drain plugs are safetyed to the engine case, there will be an eye to route the wire through. After passing the wire through the eye, ½ to ¾ of an inch more twist should be taken and the wire snipped off with a pair of side cutters. Finally, fold the wire end back on itself so the sharp points left by the side cutters don't stick out to scratch your hands. The wire will be very sharp and can cause nasty cuts. If bolts or screws are safetyed together in a series of two or more, follow the same procedure and snip and fold the twist after the last item in line.

Installing cotter keys, or cotter pins as they are also called, is not difficult if you have the proper size pin on hand and a good pair of side cutters. Cotter keys should never be reused in an airplane even though you could probably straighten and rebend a key several times before it breaks. Why risk your airplane for something as inexpensive and simple as a cotter key?

The first step in cotter key installation should be obvious—line up the hole in the bolt and nut so the key may pass through. Slide the key all the way through until the head of the key rests firmly in the receiving slot of the nut. You will notice that one end of the cotter key is slightly longer than the other. With your side cutters, grasp the longer end of the key, bend it tightly around the nut, and snip off excess length; do the same for the other end of the key. You may need to pound the key lightly with the side cutters or a small hammer to make the key ends lay tightly against the nut. Be certain the ends do not protrude to snag your skin or aircraft components.

Lubrication

We as owner-pilots are permitted to lubricate moving parts of our airplanes so long as no disassembly is required other than the removal of cover plates, cowlings, and fairings. The FARs do not specifically mention changing engine oil but they do allow cleaning of oil filter screens and since changing oil is certainly part of lubrication, this has been interpreted to mean we are allowed to change our own engine oil.

Changing engine oil is one of the few preventive maintenance procedures that will normally be required between annual inspections. Newer aircraft with full-flow oil filters normally receive oil changes every 50 hours of operation while older engines without oil filters should have the oil changed every 25 flight hours. Oil changes are not difficult to perform and require no special tools so most owner-pilots can save money by doing their own changes. But there are few items more important to an airplane's performance than engine oil. Changing oil may be simple but if you make a mistake you will no doubt find yourself flying a glider because engines do not run long without oil.

The first step in any oil change should be to buy the oil recommended by your engine manufacturer to suit present climate conditions. Each manufacturer recommends a specific weight of oil for use within an ambient temperature range. If you live up north and will be flying to the south where there are significantly warmer temperatures, select the oil viscosity weight that suits the higher temperatures you expect to encounter. Viscosity is a measurement of pourability at a given temperature and the lower the viscosity weight, the thinner the oil. Heavyweight oil will be thick and sluggish at cold temperatures but lightweight oil will thin too much at warmer temperatures and the higher engine operating temperatures warm weather causes.

Using heavier weight oil than recommended under cold temperatures can damage the engine at start-up because the oil may be too thick and congealed to flow through the engine to bearings and other lubrication points. At very cold temperature even the lightest normally used aircraft engine oil, 30 weight, will be congealed and must be preheated before the engine is started. During an engine preheat as much heat as possible should be concentrated on the engine oil sump and crankcase to warm and thin the oil for a safe start.

Multiviscosity oils are now available from several major manufacturers and are approved for use in virtually all aircraft piston engines. Multiviscosity means the oil tends to remain thinner at low temperatures but does not thin as much at operating temperature. Multiviscosity oil has been available for many years for use in automobiles but aviation multiviscosity is relatively new. The obvious benefit of multiviscosity oil is that it negates the need for seasonal oil changes as the same multiweight oil can be used year round. This is a very attractive feature for the do-it-yourself oil changer because we can buy oil in larger amounts to save money but not be forced to have more than one weight on hand to suit seasonal temperature changes.

While it is accurate to say an oil change is nothing more than draining the old oil out and pouring new oil in, the procedure is not that simple for an airplane if everything is done right. At every change the old oil should be inspected, the screen

The oil drain on most engines is often difficult to reach, as on this Cessna 182. When this plug is removed oil will run down on the carburetor, motor mount, and other assemblies and create a mess. The solution is to install a quick drain, which is a spring-loaded fitting to which a drain hose can be connected. The quick drain saves the trouble of removing and replacing with safety wire the sump drain plug and also makes the job quicker and cleaner.

checked and cleaned, and the engine reinspected after the new oil is in.

If you plan to do your own oil changes regularly, have a quick drain installed in your oil sump if it is not already there. A quick drain, as its name implies, is a spring-loaded valve that opens to allow the oil to drain out without removing any plugs or safety wire which can sometimes take as much time as the rest of the oil change.

The first step in an oil change is to run the engine until the oil is warm so it will flow freely from the sump. With the oil still warm, open the drain and let the oil run into a container, preferably covered with a fine screen that will catch any metal fragments that may have been suspended in the oil. Examine the screen for chips; if you find any metal, consult a mechanic before further flight.

The next step, cleaning the oil screen, is never easy and you will be tempted to skip the oil screen this time. For some reason oil screens are always located in the most difficult to reach position on the rear of the engine and you may have to practice some Eastern meditation to become flexible enough to reach it. The screen will be under a large nut cap, sometimes with the oil pressure or temperature transducer located in the cap.

After removing the oil screen, examine it not only for metal particles but also for the condition of the screen itself. Sometimes these fine wire screens will come apart, especially if they have become plugged with sludge, and the disintegrating screen will be sucked through the oil system it is intended to protect. Have a supply of new oil screen gaskets on hand because the last thing you want is to go to all the trouble of replacing the screen with the old gasket only to find it leaks.

If your airplane has a full-flow oil filter, it should also be replaced at oil change time. Many newer engines use the spin-on type of oil filter found on most automobiles while others use a replacement element inside a permanent container. In either case it is a good idea to dissect the old filter searching for metal fragments that may have broken off inside the engine. Be certain to safety wire the new filter in place properly but do not overtighten spin-on filters. Hand-turning of the filter will do the job without reefing down with special wrenches.

At oil change time a good shop will wash the engine down with solvent sprayed through a high pressure gun. It is essential the engine be clean so that any small oil leak will be apparent. It is unlikely you will have a high pressure solvent gun available but do the best you can to clean and keep the engine clean at all times. After the oil change is completed, warm the engine and run it up for a few minutes. After shutdown, examine the engine, especially the sump drain, screen and filter, for oil leaks.

Although the engine oil is the primary lubrication task, don't forget other moving parts such as the controls, landing gear, doors, and other hinges. Most control hinges and mechanisms can best be lubricated with an oil squirt can. You may need to remove some inspection access plates to reach control bell cranks

The oil filter on this Bonanza is the full-flow type, which is replaced entirely. Simply snip the safety wire and spin the old filter off, spin a new one in place, add safety wire, and the job is complete. It is a good idea, however, to tear the filter apart and check for any metal fragments that may have broken off inside the engine and become trapped in the filter. If you find metal fragments, show them to a qualified mechanic and have the used engine oil analyzed by a laboratory specializing in aircraft engine oil study. The metal can usually be identified and the extent of the problem determined by such an analysis.

and pushrod ends, but a few drops of oil is all that's needed to keep these parts working freely.

Many landing gear, especially retractable landing gear, have several grease fittings which should be greased with a grease gun periodically. Because the gear is always exposed to water, dirt,

Part of your lubrication program should be to grease landing gear fittings. Landing gear takes a great deal of pounding and is exposed to the moisture and dirt of the runway environment so frequent lubrication is essential.

and crud kicked up from runways and taxiways, it will probably require more lubrication than other items such as control hinges.

One area that is often overlooked during lubrication is flap tracks on those aircraft, such as the light Cessna singles that use Fowler-type flaps. The flaps should be extended and a small amount of grease applied to the tracks as recommended by the manufacturer.

Simple Fabric Patches

The FARs say an owner-pilot can make simple fabric patches not requiring rib stitching or removal of structural parts or control surfaces. That means small punctures or tears in the fabric cover may be repaired by the owner if he or she has the proper materials and sufficient knowledge.

There are still thousands of fabric-covered aircraft in use but experts in fabric covering and repair are few. What used to be a mainstay of light airplane maintenance, fabric work, is now something the average mechanic never sees. That means you will need to search out a shop with fabric experience to have work done or even to get reliable advice about what you can do yourself.

Fabric covering has become more complicated with the increasing number of coverings and coatings now in use. At one time only grade A cotton was used to cover airframes but now various forms of synthetic materials, such as Dacron or fiber glass, or combinations of those materials may be used. Paint used on fabric is commonly called dope, and comes in two common forms, butyrate or nitrate.

Specific combinations of butyrate over nitrate or cotton over synthetic may not work. In order to make a good fabric patch you must know what material is used on your airplane and what

The rear of this J-3 Cub landing gear strut has been patched and silver dope applied. The patch is simply glued into place to cover a worn spot. This is the simple type of patch any owner can perform with the proper materials.

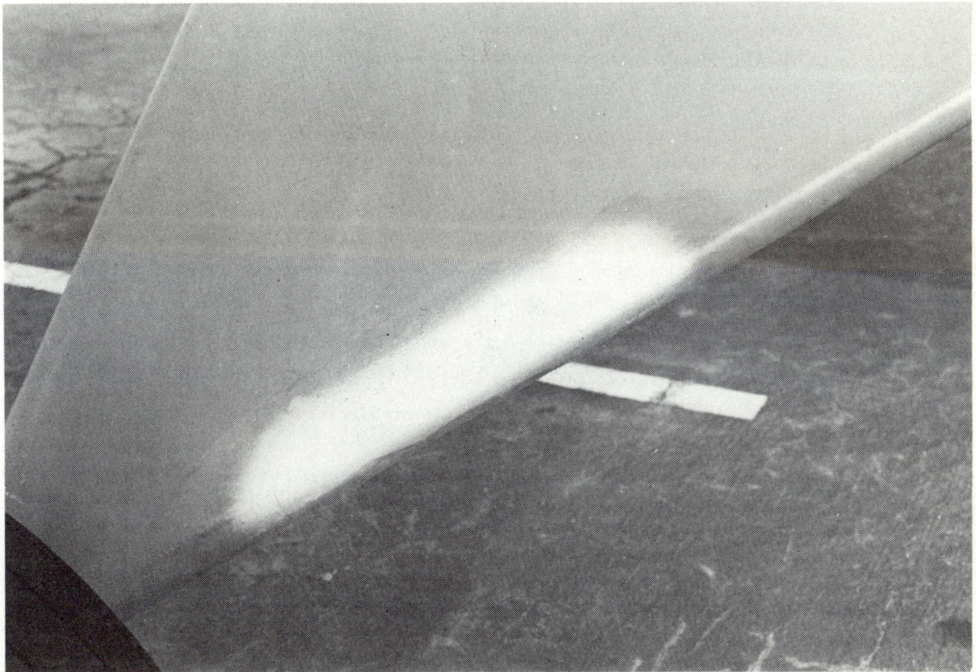

type of paint has been applied and follow manufacturer's recommended procedure for applying new dope and fabric.

Small patches such as those used to cover fabric test punch holes can be glued in place with clear dope and touched up with some colored dope. Larger patches will require the entire process of filling the fabric with clear dope, adding a coat of silver for sun ray protection, and finally matching color. Cotton fabric is shrunk taut with repeated coats of thinned clear dope but synthetic fabric is shrunk taut with heat, usually from a regular household iron.

If you are patient, careful, and willing to research the materials already on your airplane, it is possible to make small fabric patches successfully. However, replacing fabric cover is very expensive, so be certain you have all the necessary information before launching a small patch project so that it doesn't become a major re-covering job because you botched it.

Replenishing Hydraulic Fluid

Now here is a preventive maintenance procedure that should be as simple as adding air to the tires. Replenishing hydraulic fluid in the reservoir for brakes or hydraulic landing gear systems is something any owner-pilot can do. The only problem is obtaining the proper hydraulic fluid, which is the only substance that can be used in aircraft.

Mil-H-5606 is the common type of hydraulic fluid used in light airplane brakes, hydraulic gear actuators and oleo struts. The "Mil" stands for a military specification which is a uniform standard of specifications applied to such aviation materials as nuts, bolts, fittings, rivets, fluids, and the like. Although you no doubt have heard or read stories of brave and bold pilots filling an empty hydraulic reservoir with everything from booze to coffee to save a flight, use of any fluid other than that specified by the manufacturer will void warranties, be illegal in FAA eyes, and probably damage seals or other elements of the system.

Filling a hydraulic reservoir is no more difficult than pouring or squirting the specified amount of fluid into the filler spout.

Filling the hydraulic reservoir on this Piper Cherokee is as simple as pouring fluid into the small can on the fire wall. Not all hydraulic reservoirs are this easy to reach but adding fluid should not be a problem.

Finding a reasonable quantity of mil-spec fluid is another problem because most suppliers sell the fluid only by the gallon and a gallon of hydraulic fluid is more than an average light airplane owner can use up during several lifetimes. It may be better to try and buy a pint or quart of the fluid from your mechanic because that should be plenty to last through many brake or gear system additions.

If you need to add too much fluid too frequently, it is time to determine where that fluid is leaking. Small leaks in brakes or landing gear systems are often difficult to locate but if you find fluid forming in drops near a seal or fitting, the problem should be checked by a mechanic.

Refinishing Decorative Coating

Under this section of the FARs we are allowed to repaint the exterior of our airplanes but that is a job most owners will find extremely difficult to do well. The FAA again does not allow disassembly or removal of any major airframe elements such as control surfaces or parts of any primary structure. Also, only the decorative coating may be refinished, excluding the base coats of dope that protect a fabric cover from fungus and sunlight damage.

Painting any large, smooth metal machine such as an automobile requires a great deal of skill and sophisticated equipment and an airplane is even more difficult to paint than an automobile. An airplane contains every conceivable combination of curves and wide flat areas with protrusions at nearly every angle, which all adds up to a perfect showcase for painting mistakes. Another problem is that an airframe consists of many different materials. Much of the skin is aluminum alloy but many parts, such as fairings, may be made of fiberglass or other synthetic material. Preparing these various surfaces in such a way that paint will stick and flow evenly to each is a job that challenges even experts.

To paint an airplane you must have a clean, dust-free hangar with excellent lighting. A high quality paint spray gun is another must, but even the best spray gun can paint no better than the person operating it. Because the only reason you would repaint an airplane is to make it look better there is no reason to spend a great deal of your time and money and still end up with a bad-looking airplane.

However, if you wish to have your airplane painted by a professional but still want to do some work yourself to save money, you may want to strip the old paint yourself. Paint stripping is the nastiest work you will ever encounter, even worse than boat-bottom scrubbing and painting and you sailors know how bad that job is. You will need disposable clothes, patience.

and a tolerance for harsh chemicals that can take your skin off as well as remove paint.

The first step in paint stripping is to cover with aluminum foil and foil tape all windows in the airplane and anything else that you wish to protect from the paint stripper. Paper and regular masking tape will not work because the remover will eat right through the paper and attack the plexiglass windows.

Using a paint remover designed for the kind of paint on your airplane, you will be amazed how fast 90 per cent of the old paint peels off. Typically, the remover, a thick smelly potion, is brushed liberally on the old paint, allowed to loosen it, and is then washed off with a water hose. The really nasty part of the job is removing that last remnant of old paint that always sticks to joints in the skin or rivet heads or in structural formations of the skin such as the corrugations found on many airplane tails. To get rid of that last little bit of old paint you'll have to daub on more remover and scrape with a plastic scraper to avoid gouging the metal skin. Every bit of the old paint must come off if the new coat is to adhere properly and look good.

The FAA has also included one proviso that forbids an owner to paint balanced control surfaces. Technically the ailerons, elevator, and rudder on every light airplane are balanced either through mass weight, aerodynamic forces, or a combination of both. If controls are not properly balanced, they could flutter at high speeds and in extreme cases flutter can actually rip an airplane apart in flight. It is a remote possibility that unevenly applied paint could cause a control surface to exceed balance limits, but that is so remote it is nearly impossible even to imagine. But, if you want to play by the rules in every way, an owner-pilot cannot paint the flight control surfaces on his airplane. For our money painting airplanes is something best left to the professionals.

Applying Preservative Material

Just as some form of protection is necessary for the exterior of an airframe so is a preservative or protective coating ideal for the interior sections of an airframe and the FAA allows us as pilots to apply such coating so long as no major airframe assemblies or controls are removed.

The most common form of protective coating used inside an airframe is zinc chromate primer. You can buy zinc chromate in small spray cans ideal for spot spraying wherever you find corrosion or bare metal inside the airframe. Zinc chromate usually comes in either a green or yellow color and will adhere well to aluminum and combat corrosion. If corrosion has progressed to the flaky stage, remove all loose particles with a wire brush or coarse sandpaper before applying the primer.

Sometimes a light oil substance is sprayed all through the interior of an airframe to protect against corrosion but this is a process that requires special material and equipment to reach far inside wings, tails, and fuselage cones. This oily coating is desirable for seaplanes, especially those exposed to the highly corrosive effects of salt water.

The framework of fabric-covered airplanes is usually made of chrome molly steel tubing and wood and both of these materials must be protected from corrosion and rot. Steel tubing should be primed and/or painted whenever you spot corrosion

Dirt, grime, and crud have collected in the belly of this Bonanza and must be cleaned out. Dirt traps moisture and speeds the corrosive process. The belly should be cleaned and dried and sprayed with a protective coating such as zinc chromate primer.

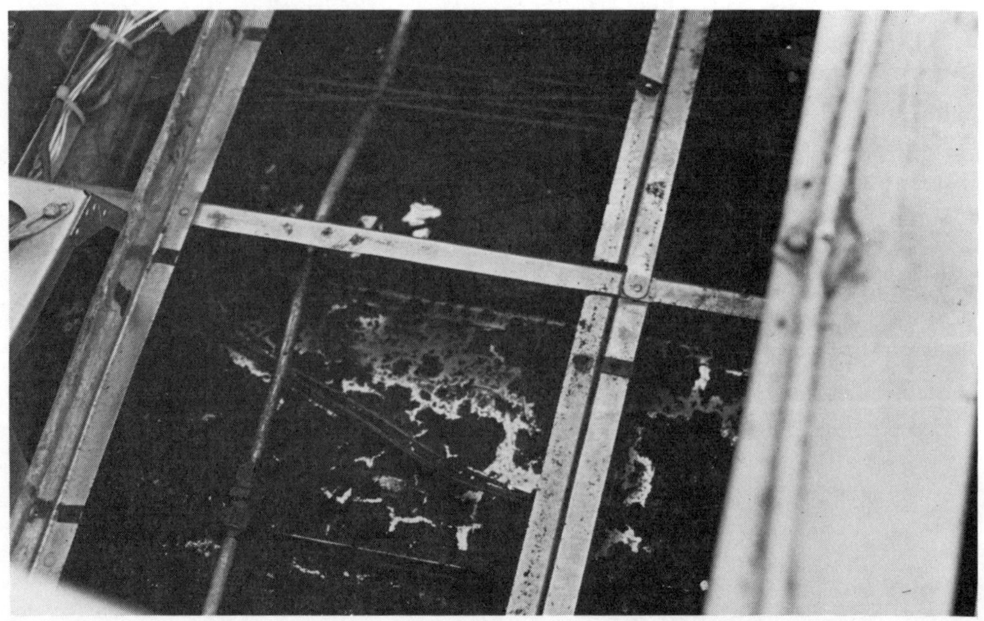

and wood components should be kept sealed with shellac or varnish to keep out moisture.

Careful attention must be directed to the belly of every airplane where dirt, moisture, and engine exhaust or oil leak residue can collect. This crud can quickly rot out a fabric cover and can cause corrosion in the belly of a metal-skin airplane. The belly and tail cone area must be kept clean and should be coated with a protective coating such as zinc chromate.

Repairing or Replacing Upholstery

Repairing or replacing upholstery is purely cosmetic work that should in no way affect the performance of an airplane unless you make a significant weight change. Any items you may add that weigh a pound or more require a new weight and balance computation and a 337 form, which must be signed by a licensed mechanic. However, most interior work we as owners may wish to perform will usually be of the replacement type.

Several manufacturers and airplane parts suppliers offer new interior components such as seat covers, door panels, side panels, and head liners. Because these items replace existing interior items there should be only a negligible weight change and it is perfectly legal for an owner to install new interior replacement parts in his own airplane.

I completely replaced the interior in my Cessna 140 using prefabricated materials from a major supplier. Although the prefab parts fit well, the job was not as easy as I anticipated. Many interior parts are glued to structure and it is difficult to get a good bond between fabric and metal. Gluing requires lengthy periods of holding panels or head liners in place waiting for glue to dry and that is tough on the arms and fingers. It is particularly disheartening to come back the next day and see the head liner you had glued in place so neatly hanging from strings of interior cement rather than tightly tucked in place as you left it.

Probably the most satisfactory interior work an airplane owner can do is replace seat covers. Airplane seats can be easily removed from the aircraft so you can work at home or in your shop. It has been my experience that prefabricated seat covers fit better than other prefab interior parts such as head liners or side panels. Also, seats suffer more wear and tear than other interior parts so new seat covers are going to make the most dramatic improvement in the appearance of your airplane cabin.

It doesn't take many years for a light airplane instrument panel to become scratched, banged up, and shabby-looking, but we can as owner-pilots refinish the panel, too. However, if we repaint or in some other way refinish an instrument panel, all control labels and placards must be replaced using exactly the same wording as was supplied from the factory. Placards are a part of an airplane's certification and must be in place for the aircraft to be legally airworthy. Something so simple as a compass compensation card is required—just the card, not the compensation values.

If your airplane is not too old and it or similar models are still in production, you probably can purchase replacement placards and control labels from the aircraft manufacturer. If the airplane is out of production, there is not much chance anyone will offer placards and labels so you will have to make your own. Aircraft supply houses offer decal assortments which contain letters, numbers, and commonly used words and phrases to make up your own placards. These decals come in various sizes and in dark or light colors to contrast with various panel shades. To stick these decals on your panel you will need a small hobby knife and plenty of patience to be certain the decals are on straight and neat, but if you are willing to spend the time, results will be very professional-looking.

Repairing Cowlings, Fairings, Etc.

The key item here is that we can repair nonstructural items ourselves provided we do not change the contour of these airframe parts. Most problems with fairings or cowlings will be cracks caused by vibration and stress or by damage from impact with rocks, hangars, or other airplanes. Our ability to repair these cracks and dings will depend largely on the type of material used to make the fairing and our skill and equipment.

The only reasonable way to repair cracks or dents in metal airframe components is to rivet patches or doubler plates over the damaged area. To do this job requires skill in metalworking, a rivet gun with compressed air to drive the gun, and metalworking tools such as snips and drills.

Cracks in sheet metal that is used on cowlings and fairings will often progress at a rapid rate if not repaired promptly. The best way to halt the progression of a sheet metal crack is to stop-drill it. That means a small hole is drilled through the sheet metal at the end of the crack and the perfect circular shape of the hole will usually stop the crack from progressing further. There are complicated metallurgical explanations for why stop-drilling works but the important fact for us is that it does work.

Stop-drilling will probably be the only repair necessary for short cracks in nonstructural sheet metal fairings but if the crack has grown to an inch or more it will almost certainly require a doubler to prevent further crack progression. A doubler is nothing more than another piece of sheet metal about the thickness of the original skin riveted behind the crack. The doubler should extend at least ½ inch on either side of the crack to allow room for rivets and to restore rigidity lost because of the crack.

Because we are allowed to make these repairs only to nonstructural fairings there are no specific rules to spell out how a patch or doubler must be fastened other than it must be done using accepted practices. The accepted practice for aircraft rivets is that A-N rivets meeting the aircraft standard be used. However, for nonstructural work many mechanics have begun using pop rivets, which require no rivet gun or bucking but are expanded by special large plier-type devices that force expansion of the rivet once it is in place. Pop rivets may be purchased at any hardware supply store and will work just fine for nonstructural repairs.

To install pop rivets, simply drill a hole, usually ⅛ inch, through both layers of metal to be riveted. The rivet is inserted in the hole, and the special tool you buy with the rivets is used to "pop" the rivet in place. Be sure to buy aluminum rivets, with flush heads so they appear less objectionable when painted over. Use only enough rivets to restore the original stiffness to the fairing and be sure the crack is stop-drilled before riveting the doubler in place.

Wheel fairings and wing tips will probably be the major source of nonstructural cracks and damage on your airplane but

The crack in this wheel fairing can be repaired with basic fiber glass repair materials. Reinforcing fiber glass and resins are applied inside the fairing to add rigidity. Noncertified mechanics are allowed to perform this type of repair because it cannot have any significant impact on flight safety.

on many airplanes these items are made from fiber glass and will require a different repair technique from metal components. Because fiber glass is nothing more than a base of fiber coated with resin you have a great deal of flexibility in making repairs and no special tools or extraordinary skill is required.

Fiber glass repair materials are available from many sources but the most likely supplier is the marine industry. Nearly all recreational boats are built from fiber glass and marine stores offer a variety of kits containing all necessary materials to repair fiber glass and gelcoat, the smooth outer coating of a fiber glass structure.

There is little advice I can add beyond following fiber glass repair manufacturers' directions, which are typically complete and easy to understand. The glass fibers used in these kits can irritate your skin, so use gloves when handling the glass material. Epoxy resins will produce powerful fumes while curing and must only be used with plenty of ventilation. Sanding, shaping, and final painting of fiber glass repairs is easy and you should have very satisfactory results.

Replacing Side Windows

Thankfully this is not a frequent repair job because window replacement in many airplanes is complicated and often demands considerable disassembly of interior side panels and trim. The FARs specifically allow owner-pilots to replace only side windows, not windshields, which can only be replaced by licensed mechanics.

The reason the FAA has reserved windshield replacement for qualified experts should be obvious. A windshield failure in flight would lead to certain disaster, but the failure of a side window would probably cause nothing more serious than a lot of noise and draft in the cabin.

All light airplane windows are made from plastic, commonly called plexiglass. Plastic is lighter than glass and more resilient to stand up to the vibration and flexing of an airframe. However, plastic is much softer than glass and must be treated with special care if it is to serve a long and useful life. Airplane windows should never be cleaned with a dry cloth because small dirt and dust particles will scratch the surface and ruin transparency. Solvents and cleaners designed for cleaning glass windows should never be used on airplane windows because many are so strong they can actually attack the surface of the plastic window, giving the plastic a foggy rather than clear appearance.

The most common form of window or windshield failure in light airplanes is called crazing and is primarily caused by sunlight and exposure to pollutants in the atmosphere. A crazed window will develop tiny surface cracks that look much like the window has been struck by an object. The cracks may either form spider web fashion or may randomly progress across the window, ruining visibility and requiring replacement.

Replacement windows are easy to obtain through aircraft parts distributors and may or may not be difficult to install, depending on the type of aircraft you own. However, dried sealant and stuck window framework can turn what should be a simple

All the screws surrounding the window on this Bonanza must be removed before the side window can be removed. Also, there is a series of screws on the inside which must come out before the window is free. Replacing side windows is not an easy task but with patience it can be accomplished.

window change into a long project of scraping and cleaning to remove the old window.

New aircraft windows are usually shipped with a paper protective covering glued to each surface. The paper should be left in place until the window installation is complete because it may be impossible to remove glue or sealant spilled on the window. Use enough sealant designed for aircraft windows to ensure a good seal free of leaks but don't overdo it with the sealer or the excess may be impossible to clean from the window and surrounding interior and exterior airframe parts.

If you have patience and basic tools, you should be able to change an airplane side window. However, before buying the replacement window, examine every detail of the job. Try to anticipate not only the interior disassembly required but other factors that may go wrong, and then decide if it is worth your time to become involved in what may turn out to be a long-drawn-out project.

Replacing Safety Belts

Installing a new safety belt should be no problem for any owner with basic tools. Most belts are bolted to the floor behind or under the seats and installing new belts involves nothing more than removing the bolts and replacing the bolts through the new belts.

However, be certain that the new safety belts you install are approved for aircraft use. Seat belts used in an aircraft look a little different and in fact are a little different from standard automotive seat belts. Be certain that the new safety belts you install are approved for aircraft use; they must have FAA approval, which will be indicated on the belt label.

Seat belts have been involved in several ADs which called for replacement, especially of the old type that used a metal buckle on one end only. Some early side-by-side two seaters like my old Cessna 140 had a common seat belt for both occupants and an AD was issued requiring replacement of this type of belt while I owned the airplane.

Replacing Seats or Seat Parts

Should your airplane seats break or wear out you can replace them provided the replacements have been approved for your specific type of airplane. Any seat that is approved will not be difficult to install because in order to gain approval it must either be identical or closely resemble the original seat. If the seat is drastically different, it must be installed under a 337 form as a major alteration with a mechanic approving the work and performing a new weight and balance calculation.

Landing Lights and Nav Lights

The FAA permits airplane owners to replace light bulbs, reflectors, or lenses in navigation and landing lights and allows owners to troubleshoot and repair problems in landing light circuits. However, it does not permit troubleshooting and repair of navigation light circuits. The only reason I can guess why the FAA calls out landing light circuits for owner repair but not navigation lights is because a landing light is not a required item for private night flight while navigation lights are required on all aircraft operated at night. In any event, most light troubles on an airplane will be burned-out bulbs or blown fuses and we are allowed to replace and repair those items.

Virtually all light airplanes used sealed beam lights for landing and taxi lights. A sealed beam light is the same type of bulb used for automobile headlights and contains both the light filament and reflector assembly. Replacing these bulbs requires nothing more than removing retaining screws and plugging in the new bulb.

Navigation lights are small bulbs shining through colored

Removing three screws frees the landing light on this Piper Cherokee for replacement. Simply remove the wires from the rear of the old light and plug in a new bulb to complete the operation.

lenses to provide the necessary red, green, or blue color. The only potential problem with replacing these bulbs is improper voltage rating with more and more light airplanes switching to a 28 volt electrical system. A 12 volt bulb will last only a few seconds with 28 volts applied so be certain to install a bulb with the proper voltage rating.

The FARs say nothing about repair of anticollision lights, such as strobes and rotating beacons, but it is safe to assume these lights fall into the bulb replacement category. However, strobe light bulbs are not something that can easily be replaced but fortunately they seldom fail. Strobe problems are usually associated with the power supply used to generate the short bursts of high voltage that give strobes their super bright light flash. If your strobes fail, check the circuit breaker or fuse. If that isn't the problem, don't fool around with the light element itself because that most likely is not the problem and you could damage

The taillight on this Bonanza is a combination nav light and anticollision strobe light. The nav light bulb is the conventional bulb in the center and the strobe element is the circular glass tube surrounding the taillight. The nav light will require replacement but the strobe light element will probably last the life of the airplane.

an expensive element of the strobe system. Strobe problems are best left to experienced technicians.

Rotating beacons do have replaceable bulbs and that could be the problem if your beacon fails. However, many times the inner contacts which transfer electrical power from the beacon base to the rotating light element either get dirty or break and are the cause of beacon failure. If your beacon has more than one bulb and both bulbs go out at once, it is usually safe to assume the problem is more serious than a light bulb failure. By removing the lens and reflector you can usually see the power transfer contacts and examine them for integrity and dirt. If the contacts are worn or dirty, you may be able to get the beacon working again by cleaning the contact points with fine grit sandpaper.

Changing from Wheels to Skis

An airplane owner is allowed to change from wheels to skis or from skis to wheels so long as the change does not result in a change in aircraft weight and balance. Changing from wheels to skis or the other way around will always change the weight and balance of an airplane but there is a legal way around that problem.

The first time a change is made a certified mechanic must fill out the necessary paperwork and compute a new weight and balance. However, once that first change has been made, an owner can change back and forth between wheels and skis legally by simply retaining the necessary paperwork and using the computed weight and balance appropriate to the airplane's current configuration.

Most skis will fit on the main landing gear axle much like a wheel and installing the skis will involve jacking up the airplane and other steps required for any wheel removal. Skis also have an elastic cord which holds the nose of the ski up in flight and a retaining cable or stop that prevents the elastic from pulling the nose of the skis too high.

Skis must be approved for your specific type of airplane and will first be installed using a 337 form for major alterations. After that paperwork is completed, a change to skis will be no more complicated than any other wheel or tire service.

Replacing Cowlings Without Removing Propeller

It seems only natural that a pilot should be able to remove the cowling from his airplane engine to inspect the engine and its systems. From our very first flying lesson the instructor hammered home the concept of a thorough preflight inspection and checking the engine for oil level, oil leaks, signs of wear, or bird nests is an important part of that inspection.

But the FARs clearly state that an owner cannot remove a propeller in order to remove a cowling and on some aircraft prop removal is necessary. The Luscombe is a more common example of a cowling that simply cannot come off unless the prop is removed and only a licensed mechanic may remove a prop. Many cowlings, however, come off in pieces and the forward section of a cowling may not be removable with the propeller in place, but most cowlings at least will come off enough to expose the top and sides of the engine.

The Bonanza series have unusual cowlings because of the uncommon keel structure of the airplane. The Bonanza has a keel section which protrudes forward from the fire wall and the engine sits on the keel rather than being mounted to the fire wall as are most light aircraft engines. Because of this keel-type construction the forward section of a Bonanza cowling does not come off and the only removable sections of the lower cowling are access panels. When you raise the hinged sections of a Bonanza cowling, you have virtually as much access to the engine compartment as you ever will. For preflight inspection the Bonanza cowl is superb with its easy-to-open hinged top sections, but when it comes to performing major engine work the permanent cowl sections and keel make the airplane more complicated than some.

Airplanes built in the past few years all tend to have tighter cowlings than earlier light airplanes as manufacturers attempt to reduce cooling drag and improve speed. Air forced over the engine to cool it in flight accounts for a significant percentage of aircraft drag and manufacturers have found tighter cowls with smaller air inlets and more efficient air flow within the cowl provide adequate cooling with improved speed. But most of these tight cowlings are built in large sections, usually with the entire top of a cowl formed in one piece. This means there are no handy hinged panels to raise for preflight inspection or minor engine work. The larger size of these cowling elements makes it difficult for a single person to install or remove the cowl because the unwieldy fairing is usually made of thin sheet metal or fiberglass and flexes like crazy when you try to put it in place and line up screw holes on two sides at once.

I operated a Piper Turbocharged Arrow for several hundred hours and wrestled with that cowling top many times. After every oil change the dipstick was invariably stuck in backward and the cowling was so tight that the only way to remove the oil

The large top section of this Piper Archer cowling is easy to remove, if you have two people. The cowling is made from fiber glass and is not only rather flexible but has proven durable in service.

dipstick through its tiny access hatch was if its design bend faced forward. The cowling would be off for the oil change, some mechanic or myself would put the dipstick in, put the cowling back on, and not realize the problem until it was time to check the oil before flight.

Many light airplanes with larger engines have cowl flaps which are used to control air flow over the engine and thus maintain engine temperatures. Cowl flaps are usually hinged to the lower trailing edge of the cowling where the exhaust stacks exit and on many airplanes the control mechanism for these flaps must be disconnected to remove the lower cowling section. The FARs do not allow the removal of any flight controls when an owner removes an engine cowling but cowl flaps are not flight controls and they may be legally disconnected by an owner-pilot.

Replacing, Cleaning, and Gapping Spark Plugs

Spark plug care and maintenance is one of those jobs that is easy—if you have the equipment. Without proper equipment it is impossible for an airplane owner to maintain spark plugs properly and the results will certainly be more costly than if left to the professionals.

Installing a new spark plug is simple if you have the necessary deep socket wrench and a torque wrench. To remove a plug, unscrew the cap which holds the lead wire into the top of the plug and remove the lead with care so the cigarette, a spring-loaded insulator, is not dropped or damaged and the plug is screwed out in the normal fashion. To replace the plug with a new one is also a snap but the plug must be tightened to the proper torque value. If a plug is screwed in too tight, it may break, or worse may strip the screw threads in the cylinder and that can mean several hundred dollars in repair work. If the plug is not tight enough, it could work loose in flight and power would be lost from that cylinder and a fire hazard would result in the engine compartment as fuel escaped from the missing spark plug hole. There are no safety wires or cotter keys to hold spark plugs in place and only correct torque tightening assures that the spark plug will not work loose.

A torque wrench is not extremely expensive and if you plan

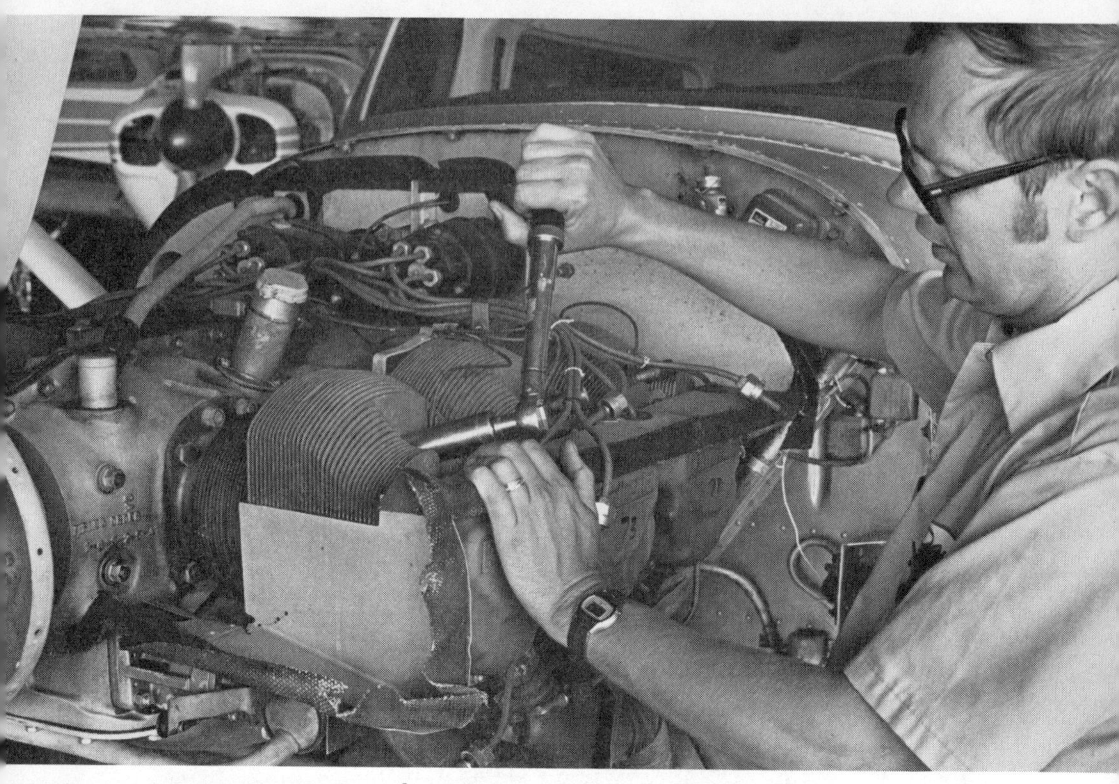

The torque wrench used to tighten a spark plug is set for the desired torque, usually 60 inch pounds, and emits a loud click when that torque value is reached. Proper torque tightening is the only way you can be assured spark plugs will neither break nor come loose.

to perform any serious work on an airplane you will need the wrench for other jobs, not just spark plug installation. But aircraft spark plugs are very expensive and if improperly handled a forty-dollar iridium element plug that is capable of lasting the entire life of an engine will be ruined.

Spark plug technology has come a long way since the FAA wrote the rules allowing owner-pilots to replace, clean, and gap their own plugs. Modern spark plugs seldom foul and required plug maintenance between annual or 100-hour inspections is unheard of.

Aircraft spark plugs fall into two major categories—massive electrode and fine wire electrode. Massive electrode plugs are similar to automotive spark plugs except there are several elements extending from the side of the aircraft plug rather than the single element found in automotive plugs. Fine wire plugs

The plug on the left is a Champion and has only two base electrodes while the AC plug on the right has three. The difference between these two brands of plugs reflects nothing more than the tradition and philosophy of the manufacturers.

have two very fine elements extending from the base to the center electrode and these fine wires are made from either platinum or iridium, an expensive metal from the platinum group.

Massive electrode plugs are the lowest in price because no precious metals are used in their construction. With good care a massive electrode plug can last 400 or 500 hours and maybe more. Platinum fine wire plugs can easily serve more than 1,000 operational hours and iridium plugs, the most expensive, often perform for the entire period between engine overhauls, which can be as much as 2,000 hours.

To obtain these long service lives, spark plugs must be properly cleaned and rotated. Cleaning requires a sandblasting machine, designed especially for aircraft spark plug cleaning, plus a vibrating cleaner. The sandblaster removes lead build-up from electrodes and the base of the plug while the vibrating cleaner is essential to remove deposits further up in the plug. A spark plug blaster and vibrator will cost several hundred dollars and could in no way pay for itself because at every annual or 100-hour inspection any good shop will clean your plugs with its machinery.

A spark plug cleaner uses compressed air to blast fine sand against the base of the plug, removing deposits without harming plug electrodes. Aircraft spark plugs are very expensive, especially the fine wire type, and you take a considerable financial risk if you attempt to clean your plugs without proper equipment.

Setting the gap clearance on an aircraft plug requires special tools. The fine wire electrodes are very brittle and can easily be broken in the gapping process if you attempt to bend the electrode without the proper tool.

Proper spark plug rotation is essential for maximum service life and any good shop will rotate plugs whenever they are removed. Aircraft magnetos have opposite polarity so when a spark plug is operating from one mag the spark will jump from the center electrode to the base and from the base electrode to the center on the other mag. The direction of spark jump is related to electrode wear so plugs are changed from one magneto to the other at each removal to even electrode wear. Also, the plugs should be moved from the bottom of the cylinder to the top because the bottom plug normally builds up more lead deposits. Proper plug rotation is from top to bottom, odd to even numbered cylinder. To ensure correct rotation, plugs must always be placed in a numbered container so you know exactly what location the plug came from. Also, if a spark plug is dropped on the concrete floor it should be discarded because the insulator inside may have cracked and the plug could fail in flight. Many shops have compression testing machines which can test spark plugs' ability to hold compression, but even these machines cannot always detect a crack resulting from a hard rap, so it is best to throw away any plug that has hit the floor.

If you fly a great deal, I recommend the fine wire plugs for maximum service life. If you only put a hundred or so hours a year on your airplane the massive electrode plugs may last as long as you intend to keep your airplane and prove more cost effective. In either case plugs are expensive and will be reliable if left to qualified personnel using proper tools and equipment.

Replacing Hoses

We are allowed to replace any hose or hose connection except hydraulic connections, which would include brakes. That means drain hoses, vacuum lines, cabin air hoses, and even static air pressure hoses can be replaced by an owner-pilot. However, no static air pressure line may be disconnected in an airplane used for IFR flight without being rechecked and recertified by a qualified mechanic. If you don't fly IFR, even static system hoses can be repaired or replaced without approval of a mechanic.

The most common cause of hose failure is chafe. If a hose hangs loosely and rubs against a moving or vibrating surface, it will chafe through and fail. The best protection against chafe is to secure all hoses tightly whenever they pass near a moving or vibrating surface and the hoses will last nearly the life of the airplane.

The general rules of any aircraft maintenance apply to hoses and hose connections so you may use only those components approved for your airplane. If you use the correct replacement parts, their installation should be easy and obvious.

The flexible hoses used to carry air for carburetor and cabin heat can wear rather quickly and according to the FARs can be replaced by an airplane owner-pilot. Hose replacement requires nothing more than clamping the new hose in place and securing it to prevent chafe.

Replacing Prefabricated Fuel Lines

Prefabricated is the key word in this clause which allows an owner-pilot to remove and replace fuel lines. A prefabricated line will have all fittings and flares in place and replacement is only a matter of tightening the fittings.

Aircraft fuel lines are usually made of metal alloy but there will normally be at least one flexible hose link between the airframe and engine to avoid metal fatigue caused by engine vibration. All fuel lines use A-N fittings, which require a double flare on the mating ends of metal lines. Double flare can be accomplished only with a special tool and that is one of the reasons we are not allowed to fabricate our own fuel lines.

It is difficult to imagine a more important line on an airplane so I recommend that you be very careful when working on fuel lines. If you have any doubts about either your ability to do the job right or the exact cause and solution to a problem, it may be worth your life to have a mechanic do it for you.

Cleaning Fuel and Oil Strainers

We discussed cleaning oil strainers in the section on lubrication and oil changes and this clause makes it clear that cleaning strainers is a legal preventive maintenance operation for the owner-pilot.

Strainers should be cleaned with solvent and blown dry with compressed air. The most difficult part of strainer cleaning will be removal of the strainers, which may be difficult to reach and require new gaskets to ensure proper seal when they are replaced.

Unless you believe you have received a load of adulterated fuel I can see no reason for cleaning a fuel strainer between annual or 100-hour inspections. The drain on all fuel strainers normally allows water and foreign matter to escape when the

The fuel strainer is rather easy to reach and remove on this Cessna 182. The strainer can be removed after the safety wire is clipped. Notice how the primary fuel line has been secured by plastic lace to prevent chafe.

strainer is drained during each preflight inspection. Careful sampling and inspection of fuel drained from the strainer is a superior procedure to unwarranted removal and cleaning of the strainer itself.

Replacing and Servicing Batteries

Replacing and servicing light airplane batteries is no different from the handling of automotive batteries. Airplane batteries are smaller, have special vent caps that seal acid in the battery during bank and pitch maneuvers, and tend to cost more than a comparable auto battery.

Battery acid level should be checked regularly and filled to the proper point with a recommended fluid, which is usually distilled water. The charge level and general health of a battery can be checked with a hydrometer, which measures specific gravity of battery acid and converts that information into an electrical charge level. If your airplane operates infrequently, it would be wise to trickle charge the battery occasionally to be certain it is up to full power, especially during the winter months when extreme cold can freeze the acid in a low charged battery and ruin it. Any of those low cost trickle chargers available at automotive supply outlets will do the job just fine.

Battery acid is very powerful and it can quickly harm people and damage the aluminum of an airplane if spilled, so be careful. All airplane batteries are housed in a sealed box that is vented overboard so any spillage of acid or fumes will be carried away from the airplane. Some few older aircraft use what is called a manifold vented battery, which has its own venting system and hose to drain away fumes or acid overflow but these batteries will normally be found only in classic airplanes.

Other than occasionally adding water or charging a battery, there is not a great deal an owner can do to save money on battery maintenance. Battery replacement is quick and simple and many times a shop will install a battery you have purchased for no extra charge. However, you may be able to shop around and find a better battery price, but be certain to buy only the type approved for your airplane. Also, beware of low prices on batteries you order through the mail because they will arrive without

Servicing batteries requires acid handling equipment to measure specific gravity of the battery acid and to add acid to new batteries. Battery acid is extremely corrosive and should be kept away from paint finishes and must be washed off quickly if it comes in contact with your skin.

acid and you must then go buy your own acid, pour it in, and charge the battery before installing it in the airplane.

More and more light single-engine airplanes are powered by 28 volt electrical systems and use 24 volt batteries so be sure you know the voltage of your airplane. A standard 12 volt auto battery charger won't do the job on a 24 volt battery.

Assembling Gliders

Most gliders, or sailplanes as they are called, are designed so that the wings or tail may be quickly removed and the airplane may be trailered behind a car or more easily stored in a hangar.

If you own a glider designed in this way, the FAA says you may remove and install the wings and tail yourself. For the rest of us the FAA says never touch any part of the primary structure that holds an airplane together.

As noted, many of the types of maintenance we are allowed to perform as owner-pilots will be impractical because of the highly specialized equipment required. One possible way to overcome this drawback is to persuade a maintenance shop to allow you to use its equipment or at least to help that shop's mechanics work on your airplane.

At one time it was not difficult to find small shops that would work with airplane owners, but sadly that picture has changed because of legal liability questions. As we noted, the mechanic who performs any work is liable for the safety of that airplane. If something on an airplane fails, the mechanic who worked on the airplane can be sued either in a civil damage case or by the FAA and in extreme cases criminal negligence charges may be possible. Because of legal uncertainty mechanics are understandably reluctant to become involved with any airplane work over which they have anything less than total control. There is a possibility that by allowing an owner-pilot to use tools, equipment, or to perform his own work on shop premises, a mechanic could assume some legal liability for the work, so co-operation from a shop will not come easy.

The only possible way to gain the aid of a mechanic is to become his friend and earn his trust. Spend time at the shop and try to learn about work being done on your airplane but don't get in the way and tie up work, especially if the mechanic is working on some airplane other than your own. Every minute of a mechanic's time must be accounted for so if you waste his time by asking questions while he is working on another airplane, the owner of that airplane will pay the tab for your answered questions.

When your airplane goes in for routine service, whether it is an oil change or inspection, ask if you can help. Removing inspection plates, cowlings, and interior components to ready the airplane for inspection are procedures you as owner are allowed to perform and the mechanic may be agreeable to allowing you to take these steps in his shop. Bring your own tools because no mechanic ever wants his tools spread around, they simply disappear too often. Work quietly without disturbing other mechanics and do careful neat work if you expect this arrangement to continue.

If you do good work during an inspection, the mechanic may allow you to help in more complex procedures. For example, the wheels must come off to be checked and have the bearings packed with grease. The mechanic can show you how to disassemble the brake for wheel removal, a procedure we as pilots cannot do, and then you can do the dirty work of cleaning and greasing. Other steps in the inspection often require a helper for the mechanic and you may be helpful and save some money in that way. For example, during a compression check the prop must be firmly held when the test air pressure is applied to prevent it from rotating and this is a job we all can do. Bucking rivets often takes two people as does installing large one-piece engine cowlings and many other steps and you may be able to help in those ways.

When I owned my Cessna 140 I became close friends with a mechanic in a small shop and he would allow me to help during inspections and perform many routine tasks. In theory I was being charged only for the hours spent on the airplane plus parts and materials but it seemed that whether I helped on an inspection or not, the bill was about the same. However, those inspections I worked on were all complicated with several squawks to solve and if I had not done the dirty work of inspection plate removal and so on myself, the bill would have been much higher. I was lucky to find a mechanic happy to work with owners and teach them about their airplanes but not all mechanics are that way. In fact, I have seen shop rate signs posting one hourly rate for service and a rate double the normal if the owner wants to watch and ask questions. Although those signs are usually an attempt at humor, they do reflect the attitude of many mechanics who find it difficult to work with someone looking over their shoulder. If you take your airplane to such a person, leave him alone to do his work because you won't save a dime by "pitching in" yourself. If you really want to work on your own airplane and learn what makes it function, keep looking for a co-operative and helpful mechanic who will teach you and let you in on the action.

5

Major Engine Repair and Overhaul, the Most Expensive Part

Most pilots love to hear an airplane engine smoothly ticking away but if you own an airplane, that ticking may sound more like a time bomb waiting to explode and take your bank account with it. Major engine repair is a large expense every airplane owner faces. Probably the greatest expense any of us will encounter as airplane owners.

The most troubling aspect of major engine maintenance for many owners is the unpredictable nature of engine problems. It is highly unlikely that an engine will fail in flight. Very few engines quit in operation for reasons other than fuel starvation or induction ice and that excellent record is due primarily to rigid inspection requirements. It is during those annual or 100-hour inspections that the bad news of pending engine problems will most likely be discovered.

Of course, every airplane owner has read of the concept of engine manufacturer's recommended time between overhaul (TBO). Most engines used in light airplanes now have a TBO of at least 1,400 operational hours and many engines are capable of 2,000 hours of operation between overhauls. Those figures represent well over ten years of flying by the average private light airplane owner and should be comforting rather than frightening, but TBO is not an absolute and only a minority of engines reach recommended TBO without major repair along the way.

The concept of TBO is based on regular use and strict adherence to operation and maintenance procedures. If you don't fly the fifteen hours a month engine manufacturers recommend for long engine life, reaching TBO is unlikely. The same goes for deviation from operational recommendations such as specified warm-up procedures and avoidance of rapid cooling during descent. The point is, TBO life is not what we should expect from an engine but what we can hope for as the best possible life expectancy if everything goes perfectly.

Most of us are going to encounter the need for top overhauls of at least a few cylinders before reaching engine TBO limits and many engines will require major overhauls well before TBO life has expired. Each time an engine problem crops up during an inspection the owner has several options of exactly how to correct the problem and will often receive conflicting or confusing advice from shops and friends. There are several terms used to describe major engine work and not every owner or mechanic means the same things when they say the engine has been "topped" or "majored" so the owner or prospective owner must be certain to determine exactly what work has been performed on the engine and not simply be guided by general categories.

The Top Overhaul

Cylinder problems are the most common failure of airplane engines and are usually discovered during compression checks taken at every annual or 100-hour inspection. Piston rings frequently fail by cracking or sticking in their seats. Cylinder valves, especially the exhaust valves, are the most common cylinder problem because they can burn or wear to the extent that sufficient compression is no longer developed in a cylinder. Whenever any of these problems is corrected the procedure is commonly called a top overhaul.

Unlike most automotive engines where the cylinders are part of a cast metal case, airplane engine cylinders are bolted to the engine case as independent units. Several types of metal and metal alloys are used in an airplane engine to save weight where possible so an entire engine could not be made from a single casting. Even the cylinders themselves, often called jugs, are typically made with steel barrels and an aluminum alloy head, providing the strength and wear resistance in the cylinder itself but with an aluminum head to save weight.

Because cylinders are independent from the engine and from each other, problems in individual cylinders can be corrected without removing other cylinders or the engine itself. Removing a cylinder is not extremely difficult for a qualified shop. A new cylinder or a reworked jug can be replaced in a matter of hours and the engine returned to service if time is the most important factor. Usually the defective cylinder can be repaired and replaced if the owner is willing to allow his airplane to sit and wait the few days or more it takes to have the cylinder problem corrected.

Most smaller repair shops will not have the equipment nec-

A cylinder has been removed from this Cessna 337 engine for reconditioning. The engine itself is not removed but the airplane is out of service while the defective cylinder is rebuilt. Even though only one cylinder is being reworked, some less than accurate aircraft salesmen could say this engine has received a complete top overhaul.

essary to rework a defective cylinder completely but will send the unit to a facility specializing in cylinder repair. However, it is an owner's decision whether the minimum repairs should be made or whether the cylinder should be entirely rebuilt or replaced.

Typically the valves will be culprits in low compression. Strong double springs hold the mushroom-shaped valves tightly against their seats to seal engine compression. Wear of the valve itself or the valve seat will cause a compression leak and may be corrected by grinding a new surface on the valve and seat. A more serious valve problem is stem wear or valve guide wear. The valve guide is a metal tube which, as its name implies, guides the valve stem as it moves in and out with every other piston stroke. If the guide or stem wear, the valve can move laterally in its seat and if movement is large enough the valve can

This mechanic is pointing to a very unusual valve failure—the exhaust valve is frozen in the open position. Valves can often stick in the guide but this valve is frozen in the full open position and must be pressed out and replaced along with the valve guide.

break during engine operation. The term for this catastrophe is "sucking a valve" because that is exactly what the engine does with the fractured valve, it sucks it into the cylinder and the results are usually a destroyed engine and possibly a destroyed airplane due to sudden power loss.

In some cases the mechanic will know exactly what has failed inside a cylinder before it is removed but more commonly the exact nature and extent of a problem cannot be determined until the cylinder is off and disassembled. The mechanic is obligated to repair anything he finds wrong but it is up to the owner to decide if all worn parts should be replaced or only those parts worn beyond tolerance limits. If you intend to keep the airplane for more than a few more months I recommend the cylinder be totally reconditioned no matter what problem was found once the cylinder was removed.

A rebuilt or reconditioned cylinder will be cleaned and checked for cracks using dye penetration or some other sophisticated method. Valve guides and seats will be pressed from the cylinder and new guides and seats pressed in. If valves are in good condition, they may be ground to a new smooth surface but most likely will be replaced. Finally, the cylinder barrel itself will be checked for roundness and wear and if it measures out of manufacturer's tolerances it will be chrome-plated inside to restore original shape and size. Unlike drag racers and other hot rodders in cars, chrome on airplane cylinders goes inside, not outside. On the inside the chrome can provide a long-wearing surface for piston rings to work against and can be applied to restore nearly perfect shape and size to the cylinder barrel itself.

The piston for each cylinder removed will also be cleaned and examined and may require replacement. In any case, new piston rings, possibly slightly oversized to compensate for cylinder wear, will be fitted during the cylinder rebuilding process. Once the job is complete the cylinder should be as good as new and hold compression as well as cylinders in a new engine.

The decision on rebuilding or replacing only a defective cylinder or all cylinders should be based on engine time since last overhaul, the condition of other cylinders, and the length of time you intend to own the airplane. Cylinders can fail at any time during engine life and if one goes bad with only a few hundred hours on an engine since new or last overhaul, only that defec-

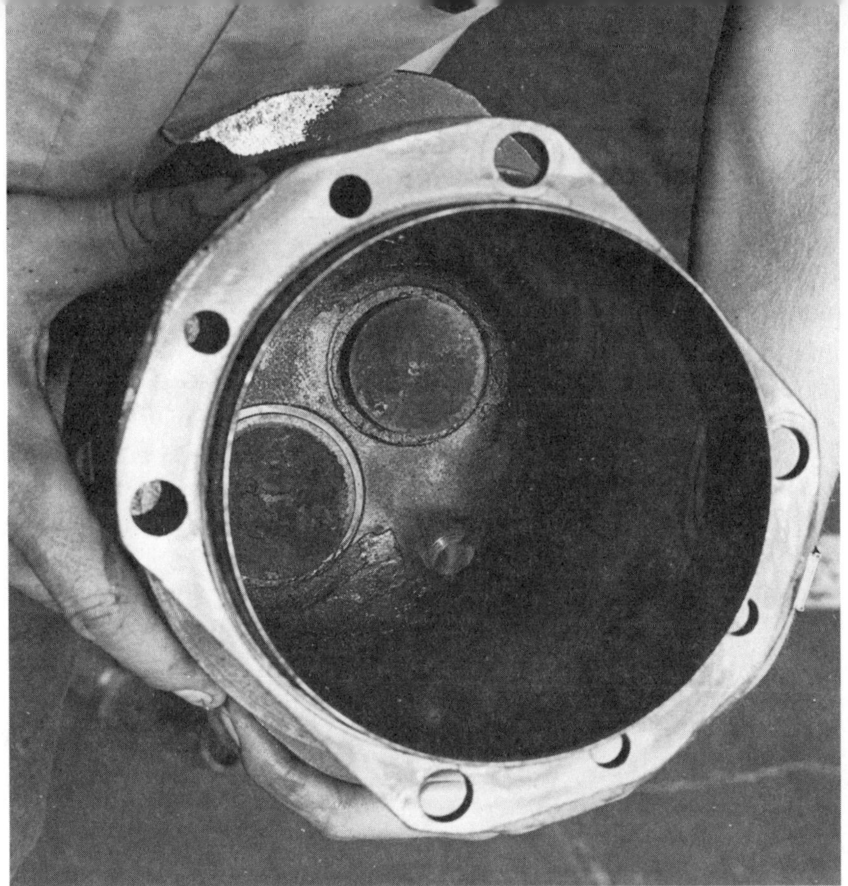

This is what an airplane engine cylinder looks like inside. The smaller valve on the left is the exhaust valve. The small hole on the right is for one of the spark plugs.

tive cylinder should be removed and repaired. If an engine has gone past the midpoint of its TBO and a cylinder fails, the decision will be more difficult and must be based on the condition of other cylinders on the engine. If other cylinders hold good compression, the engine does not use an abnormal amount of oil, and close inspection can detect nothing more than normal wear, it would probably be a waste of money to top all cylinders simply because one failed. However, if compression is on the low end of acceptability on other cylinders, placing a new, high compression cylinder into the firing order is not a good idea because it could create additional vibration by developing more power than its partners.

Many mechanics object to top overhauling cylinders on an engine that has used up 75 per cent or more of its TBO life. Their reasoning is that the new cylinders will develop power at the new engine level but other primary internal engine components such as the crankshaft and connecting rods will be worn to an unknown extent and be subjected to the restored power of the topped cylinders. I personally don't agree with this argument for most light airplane engines because primary structure failures such as broken piston connecting rods and crankshafts are rare and do not appear to be directly related to engine time in service. The argument is no doubt valid for larger piston engines which put out over 300 horsepower, but for smaller engines found in many light singles I believe the threat of a catastrophic internal failure remains approximately the same throughout engine life.

High time airplane operators who fly more than 200 hours each year may find it uneconomical to perform top overhauls except when a single cylinder fails early in engine life. If you use your airplane a lot, the downtime required for top overhaul may

This logbook entry details the removal and reconditioning of an engine cylinder. Notice the return to service tag supplied by the engine shop which rebuilt the cylinder.

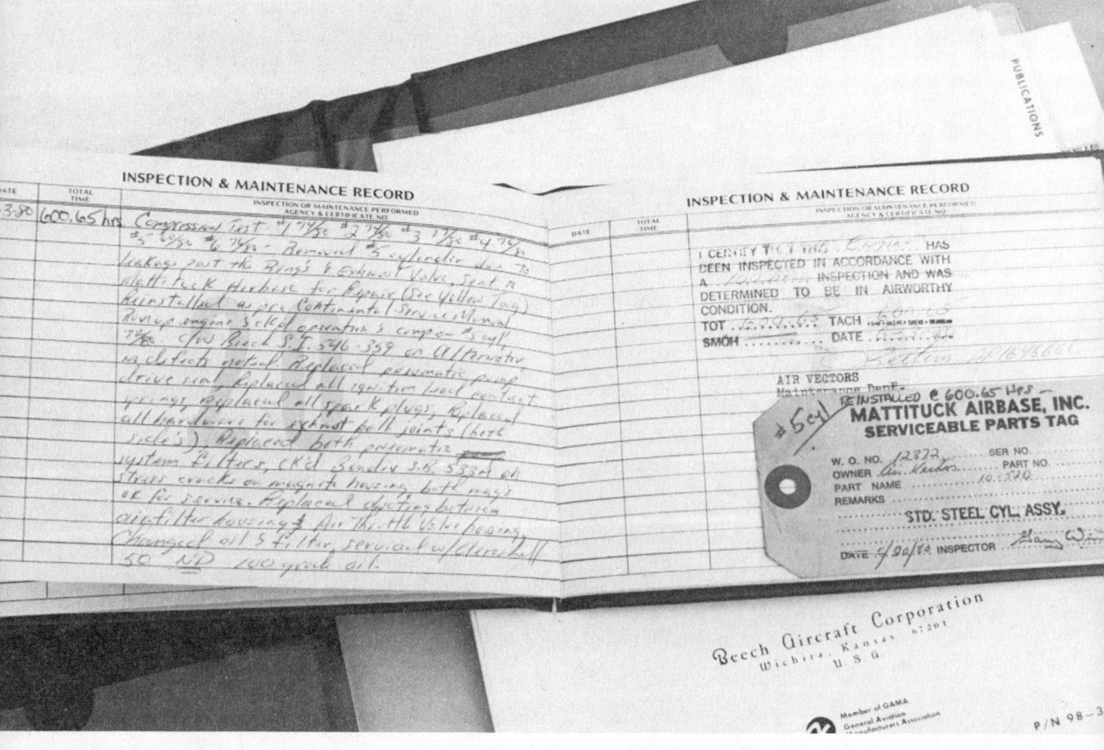

prove more costly than simply taking the same downtime to perform a major overhaul or engine exchange. Topping cylinders one or two at a time may not save a great deal when viewed over the long term but for the average light airplane owner who flies 100 to 150 hours a year a topped cylinder could easily get the engine through another year or two of flying before major overhaul is required or another cylinder requires work.

The top overhaul is a favorite of used airplane salesmen because it brings compression up during inspection and gives the salesman that key word of "overhaul" to impress on the prospect. If you are on the selling end, a top overhaul to some extent may well pay for itself by increasing the value of your airplane and moving it faster to a new owner. From the purchasing end, be sure to find out what work was done during the top overhaul by searching the maintenance records, or better yet paying a knowledgeable and reliable mechanic to search the records for you. Topping one or two cylinders means nothing except problems in those cylinders that were corrected so the engine could pass inspection. If all cylinders have been rebuilt by a reliable and reputable firm, you have good assurance that impending cylinder problems have been held at bay for some time and most likely the engine will be able to finish out its TBO. The key is that the cylinders be rebuilt by a reputable shop with all new or reconditioned valves, seats, guides, and rings and that all cylinders have been included.

Major Overhaul

The term "major overhaul" sounds inclusive but like a top overhaul a major can take many forms and have many meanings to different people. Reduced to its most basic definition, an engine has been fully disassembled in a major overhaul and certain wear-out components such as bearings and piston rings have been replaced. At the top end of the spectrum, a major overhaul can include all new moving engine parts except the crankshaft, creating an engine that is really as good as new.

An airplane engine requires a major overhaul when inspection reveals some problem within the engine that cannot be repaired by cylinder overhaul. Low oil pressure due to bearing wear, metal chips in engine oil, and operational time at recommended TBO are typical reasons for majoring an engine. As I noted, most engine problems such as low compression, valve leaks, or high oil consumption will be cylinder problems that can be solved by top overhauling an engine. However, internal engine problems such as worn piston connecting rods, crankshaft wear, or crumbling crankshaft or rod bearings cannot be cured by a top overhaul and are the types of problems which can lead to sudden engine stoppage. That is simply another way of saying rod or crank failures are usually sudden and wipe out engine power completely.

Manufacturer's recommended TBO exists in a gray legal area. TBO is only a recommendation so the FARs do not require an engine to be majored when operational hours since manufacture or since last overhaul reach TBO. However, operating an engine well beyond its TBO even though it continues to pass 100-hour or annual inspections may not be considered responsible operation by your insurance company and that could be a hassle if the engine quits causing an accident. But if the engine has been signed off by certified A&P or IA as appropriate, the airplane is legal to fly no matter if it has exceeded TBO.

Operating an engine beyond its TBO life without a major is a problem most of us will not have to deal with because only a minority of engines reach TBO without requiring major overhaul. Should your engine come up to TBO and still pass inspection you must rely on the judgment of your shop. There is no reason to tear down an engine that is functioning properly but the first hint of trouble signals it's time for a major overhaul.

There are several ways to rejuvenate your engine through major overhaul, each with its advantages and drawbacks. I cannot say which method of major overhaul suits your operation best but can explain each option so you can decide.

The first option to consider is having your shop perform the major overhaul in-house. Many smaller shops will not get involved with majors because they simply do not have the equipment. Even if the shop claims to be equipped for and have the staff to perform a major, take a look around and see for yourself. Avoid any "shade tree" operations even though they will no doubt offer the lowest cost estimate.

To perform a satisfactory major overhaul a shop must have a

separate engine room where the engine will be disassembled and cleaned. Look at this facility and examine it for cleanliness and good order of parts and subassemblies. Talk to the engine mechanics and attempt to gain some insight into their experience with and knowledge of your particular engine.

A small shop will invariably send out the cylinders and probably the crankshaft for rework so be certain any shop you consider uses a reliable aviation engine repair shop for its subcontract work. Small shops may also have to send out any crankcase parts that require ultrasonic or X-ray testing and welding as these operations require expensive and specialized equipment.

The cost estimate from a small shop will probably be the lowest you will receive but may also be the most inaccurate and least complete. Because small shops do not perform major overhauls with regularity they will not be as familiar as large shops with your specific type of engine. They will not know the probable condition of major components such as the crankshaft or the cylinders. The estimate could include only the basics, such as new bearings, piston rings, and valves, but in reality your type of engine may typically require many more new parts.

Just as a small shop cannot accurately predict overhaul costs, it cannot predict downtime, either. Because all major reconditioning of cylinders and crankshafts will probably be sent to contract shops, the small repair facility will be at the mercy of these suppliers and because it uses these suppliers infrequently, your engine parts go to the bottom of the list.

Now that I have listed the drawbacks of a small shop major overhaul, let's consider possible benefits. First, many small shops are run by experienced mechanics who will take a personal interest in your airplane, in you, and certainly in their work. There is no substitute for careful workmanship during an overhaul. Often the small maintenance shop can do a major overhaul at lower cost than large engine specialists because the small shop has lower overhead, contracts out more work, and is under less time pressure to deliver. If aircraft downtime is not paramount to you, the potentially lower price may make the small shop overhaul attractive. However, in no circumstance should you serve your engine up as a guinea pig. Find out if a shop you are considering has overhauled engines of your type, try to talk to the owners of those engines and determine the quality of workmanship. The

This crankshaft is nothing more than scrap after it has been tested and found defective. The tag identifies the crank as unserviceable and the dark paint on the crank journals indicates defective areas.

lowest cost overhaul is the engine that delivers the most time in service for dollars spent, not the overhaul with the lowest total bill.

If you fly your airplane more than 250 hours a year, I would not consider a small shop overhaul because the aircraft would be out of service for too long. Instead, one of the many engine specialists should be able to overhaul your engine and get you back in the air in a few days.

Leading engine overhaul shops offer two types of major overhaul—the exchange or rebuilding of your own engine. As the word implies, if you buy an exchange, you trade your engine for one that has been newly majored and the only time the aircraft is out of service is the length of time required to remove existing engines and bolt reconditioned engines in place, usually a matter of no more than two days. To overhaul your own engine the major shops will remove it from the airplane and send it down their assembly-line type of overhaul process; that same engine will be reinstalled.

Obviously, the engine exchange offers the fastest possible way to rejuvenate a worn engine. The engine is not the engine you have been flying with but is one that has either all new or reconditioned parts that the overhaul center certifies meet FAA standards. The reconditioned parts, such as crankcase and crankshaft, have come from other engines traded in. When your engine goes in on the exchange it is called a carcass. Usually the crankcase and the crankshaft are the only major parts reused without significant rework. Cylinders typically must be chrome-plated back to tolerances and pistons, valves, and other subcomponents are replaced.

Despite the fact that parts are reconditioned, inspected, and certified to be within tolerances, some pilots simply don't like the idea of an engine exchange. They want the same engine that has kept them flying back in the airplane even though most of the moving parts will have been replaced or reconditioned. The argument is that you know the history of your engine, how it has been maintained and how it has performed, but with an exchange engine you know nothing of its past. In my view pilots should not fear an exchange engine because no engine overhaul is any better than the shop that performed the work and stands behind it. If the shop does shoddy work, having your own engine overhauled is no better than exchanging it for another. But if you feel strongly that you want your own engine overhauled and returned, any major shop will be happy to accommodate you but at the price of longer aircraft downtime.

Business and Commercial Aviation magazine has reported that no more than half a dozen major engine overhaul and exchange shops account for the largest share of field overhauls. Because these shops are so competitive and established they are able to offer the airplane owner not only a good overhaul but many other benefits, such as warranties beyond what a small shop can give and more accurate estimates of cost and downtime. To preserve their reputations, these shops will not scrimp on an overhaul and attempt to reuse marginal parts. Shops like Schneck, T. W. Smith, Mattituck, Western Skyways, Piedmont, and others, put their name, reputation, and warranty on every engine they overhaul. Probably a major shop will not give the lowest price, but initial overhaul price is not a valid measure. The only real price is the number of operational hours an overhaul provides and with major shops you can have good assurance, maximum service life will be achieved.

If you are willing to settle for nothing but the best in engine overhauls, the only place to send your engine is back to the factory. Only original engine manufacturers are certified by the FAA to overhaul, rebuild, or remanufacture, as it's called, an engine to true zero time. All engines returned to the factory for rebuild are rebuilt and only those parts which meet new engine specifications are used; all others are replaced with new parts. Because every part of the engine is either brand new or meets the brand-new specifications and the work has been performed by the company that originally built it, the FAA declares the engine as good as new. A factory rebuild gets a new serial number, a new logbook, and a new warranty. It is in every way as good as new.

Factory rebuilt engines are also sold on an exchange basis much the way a major engine shop does. Whenever you exchange your engine a specific allowance will be made for the old engine but you must certify that the crankshaft and crankcase can be reused. Of course, we pilots have no way of knowing if a crankshaft is good or not but the exchange price will be based on a good case and crank. If, when the engine is disassembled, those components cannot be reused, you will pay more for the exchange. Obviously, if our old engine cannot be rebuilt, we have nothing to exchange and will be buying a rebuilt or reconditioned engine from the manufacturer.

During any major overhaul you will have to deal with the problem of accessories. Applied to engines the term accessories can be very misleading for most pilots because engine accessories are not really optional items like paint stripes or chromed valve covers. Magnetos, carburetors, alternators, starters, and turbochargers are all considered accessories on an airplane engine even though the engine cannot operate without those components. Try running an engine without mags or a fuel system.

When you go shopping for an overhaul discuss accessories and how they will be handled. Mags, fuel systems, and even starters and alternators should be cleaned and rebuilt at major overhaul time. These subsystems may be performing well but it is not efficient to put worn mags or fuel systems on what is essentially a new engine. Turbocharger systems are especially important because they operate at very high temperatures and rotation speeds and often wear out before the engine itself. The point is that accessories should be included in any overhaul and the price and downtime estimate must reflect that fact. If you receive an overhaul estimate well below others there is a good chance accessories are being given short shrift or may not be included at all.

If your airplane has a variable pitch or constant speed propeller, that will also have a TBO and should be considered at engine overhaul time. Prop TBO does not always coincide with engine TBO but unless the engine has suffered a premature failure, it is probably most effective to have the prop and prop governor overhauled when the engine is down for its overhaul.

Any major prop work such as an overhaul must be done by shops with FAA prop repair certification. Many of the leading overhaul/exchange facilities have both engine and prop certifica-

The blades of this turbocharger compressor have been damaged by some form of foreign object ingestion. The compressor fan may be replaced and the rest of the turbocharger reused but in any case this will be an expensive accessory added to engine overhaul price.

tion and may do both jobs in-house. Small shops will send your prop out for service.

All controllable pitch props now built use engine oil pressure to control prop blade pitch. Earlier props sometimes used electrical actuators and some even used mechanical means to adjust the blade angle of attack but those methods were abandoned years ago and most electric or mechanical props have been replaced by hydraulic units controlled by oil pressure.

Virtually all controllable props flying today are constant speed props, which means the pilot selects an engine rpm value and a governor controls oil pressure to the prop so engine speed is maintained during power changes and aircraft angle of attack changes. Prop governors also have a recommended TBO and usually should be overhauled or at least examined when the prop goes in for service.

A constant speed prop is made of two major subelements—

Oil under pressure from the engine flows into this prop hub to control blade pitch. Wear around the hub bearings and leaks in hub oil pressure seals are the common problems of constant speed props as they near overhaul time.

the hub and the blades. The hub contains hydraulic pressure actuators and flyweights to control blade pitch and bearings and seals to hold the blades and oil pressure in place. The most common wear to a prop hub is to the seals which contain oil under pressure although the entire unit will be tested for cracks or metal fatigue that could lead to a catastrophic failure and loss of a prop blade in flight. When prop hub seals wear they can leak and oil will fly out and be found on the blades. However, if you find an oily substance on your prop blades be certain it is engine oil and not grease before pushing the panic button. Prop hubs are greased during routine engine inspection and if the mechanic applies too much grease it will fly out and stick to the blades. If you find grease on the blades, don't worry, but if the substance is engine oil, have the prop examined by a mechanic before further flight because a leak in the prop seal could cause a prop failure leading to an engine overspeed. On single-engine airplanes with constant speed props a loss of oil pressure in the prop hub will cause the flyweights to pull the prop to extreme low pitch and in normal flight the engine will exceed its maximum rpm if the pilot does not quickly pull the throttle back.

Propellers used on light twin-engine airplanes are of the full feathering type. In the feathered condition prop blades rotate 90 degrees to the airplane flight path to eliminate wind resistance and allow the engine to stop turning in the event of an engine failure in flight. Most feathering props use gas pressure in the prop hub dome to push the blades into the feathered position. Should that gas leak out, the prop will not feather and a light twin cannot perform up to its engine out potential with the dead engine windmilling. In fact, most light twins will not climb and may not even hold level flight under many conditions with an engine windmilling. For that reason light twin owners must be even more conscious of prop condition and adhere to overhaul schedules.

Most disastrous prop failures occur in the blades. Blades can break, causing an extreme imbalance which many times vibrates the engine to such a degree that it is ripped from the airplane. Once the engine falls off most airplanes are so far out of CG limits that they will not glide and catastrophe is the only result.

Nearly all prop blade failures can be traced to nicks in the blade caused by striking a rock or other hard object. The outer 18 inches of a prop blade is the most critical location for a nick or scratch in the metal because that portion of the blade is exposed to the most extreme bending and vibration loads. The FAA defines minimal damage as surface nicks or scratches on the leading edge, trailing edge, or blade surface. Minimal nicks can be found on any prop and can be filed smooth by a certified mechanic. Pilots are not allowed to perform any prop maintenance and that includes filing, sanding, or painting of the blades. Even minimal damage nicks which show no measurable penetration of the blade surface must be repaired by certified mechanics.

The next degree of blade damage is moderate and a nick or scratch can be as much as 3⁄16 inch deep and still be classified as moderate damage by the FAA. An A&P mechanic can repair moderate damage but near blade tips a 3⁄16-inch nick may exceed the prop manufacturer's minimum thickness requirement when it is repaired. Severe damage may not be repairable or may require the blade to be clipped, which can be done within limits but only by a certified repair station.

During a prop overhaul, a prop shop will remove all nicks and scratches to blade edges and surfaces and check to be certain the blade is within minimum tolerances. Nicks that are too deep mean the blade must be thrown away and replaced. Finally, the prop will be reassembled and balanced by adding weight in the hub or removing metal from a heavy blade. All overhauled props, whether fixed pitch or constant speed, should receive some form of sophisticated crack inspection such as dye penetration to be certain almost invisible damage is not present.

Once your major engine overhaul and prop overhaul are completed and the airplane is ready to fly, remember you are operating an essentially new power plant and that means following a strict break-in schedule. Most overhauled engines will use non-detergent mineral oil for the first 50 hours to allow new bearings, rings, and other moving parts to wear in quickly. Be careful that some line service man doesn't add detergent oil to your engine during this period because the detergents could disrupt the break-in process. It is usually a good idea to put a tag on your engine oil filler cap during break-in, reminding anyone who adds oil that only straight mineral oil may be used. Power settings will

This prop blade has sustained at least moderate damage and may require a blade tip clip. A certain amount of metal can be clipped from prop blades to remove damage but that work can only be performed by a certified prop repair shop.

also be critical during break-in, with most overhaul shops and manufacturers recommending high cruise power settings and very gradual warm-ups and cool-downs during the first 100 hours. After paying many thousands of dollars for an overhaul, don't risk your money by deviating from break-in recommendations.

6

Airframe Problems You Can Expect and How to Solve Them

Airframe maintenance will not be as costly, regular, or predictable as engine repair but can crop up and wreck your checking account for months.

Most airframe problems will fall into the "three C" category —cracks, corrosion, or controls. I estimate that 75 per cent of all airframe maintenance costs will be spent on these three problem areas.

Cracks can appear in any part of the airframe and are obviously the most dangerous problem because they can rapidly lead to a structural failure. All substances, metal, wood or man-made material such as fiber glass, have finite fatigue lives. The constant vibration and flexing of an airframe can flex the metal or other materials beyond the fatigue life limits and a crack starts. We have all experienced this phenomenon by bending a coat hanger back and forth until it snaps. Obviously, airframes do not make such drastic bends or flexes, but the flexing and vibration of bumpy flights have the same effect.

Corrosion is a problem for every metal structure whether it is an aircraft, automobile, boat, or building. Many pilots believe that because aluminum will not rust, corrosion is not a problem. Nothing could be further from the truth. Next to cracks and crashes nothing can shorten the life of an airframe faster than corrosion.

Controls are a source of airframe maintenance problems because they are moved by a complex set of cables and pushrods and suspended on bearings which wear. Control surfaces can be placed under extreme loads. For example, all aircraft have a maximum flap extension speed because if flaps are extended at a higher speed they may simply be blown away by air pressure.

Dealing with Cracks

Because airframe cracks can be catastrophic, every IA will be looking more for cracks than any other single problem during an inspection. The wise pilot will look just as closely before each flight because cracks can easily develop between annual inspections and any new crack in a structural surface should be examined by a certified mechanic as soon as possible.

Cracks typically must have a starting source, such as a rivet hole, the edge of a metal piece, a metal-to-metal joint, or the junction of two differing types of material. It is very unusual to find a crack in the middle of a metal structure such as a piece of wing skin. The crack will have both a source and a conclusion and will progress between those points if left unrepaired.

Cracks in metal skin are not generally difficult either to spot or repair. Trailing edges of controls, flaps, or cowlings seem to generate cracks for no apparent reason. A nick in the edge of the metal is enough to get these little cracks going and they will proceed from the trailing edge to the next hard point such as a rivet line or spar line. Skin cracks are usually stop-drilled. That is, a small hole, usually about ⅛ inch in diameter, is drilled in the skin directly at the end of the crack to stop crack progression. Round holes will stop cracks or prevent crack generation. A hole of any other shape in metal skin will generate a crack and that is why even rectangular cutouts in airframes must have the corners rounded with a drill or file.

The FARs permit any pilot to make repairs of cracks on nonstructural airframe elements such as cowlings, wheel parts, or inspection covers if we do not change the contour of these airframe parts. If the crack is short, less than 1 inch, stop-drilling should be enough to solve the problem.

Should a crack progress 1 inch or more it usually will require installation of a doubler to prevent further cracking. Long cracks allow the skin to flex and even stop-drilling won't be enough to stop this, so the doubler is needed to halt skin flexing.

Stop-drilling will be required in any case and the doubler is nothing more than another piece of metal riveted under the crack to support the original skin. The doubler should be made of the same thickness as the original skin and must extend beyond the crack in all directions. Rivets cannot be too close to the crack or to the trailing edge of the skin to be repaired or new cracks between rivet holes may develop.

Cracks of a more serious nature are usually found in primary structure items such as spars, motor mounts, landing gear components, or control bearing supports. All of these airframe items are made from metal much thicker than skin surfaces and a crack in thick metal usually leads to a rapid, total failure. Stop-drilling does not work on thick metal or cast metal and replacement of the cracked part is required.

Cracks in heavy metal components are not easy to find for most of us but good mechanics or IAs can spot them quickly. One year my old Cessna 140 was in for an annual inspection and the IA saw a crack in the motor mount when he walked by on his way to the lunchroom. Even after he pointed out the crack in the cast metal part, I was unable to see it clearly. When the inspection took place, he spotted another hairline crack, this time in the lower rudder bearing support. If either of these cracks had not been located and the parts not replaced, the engine and/or rudder could have fallen off in flight and I would not be here to write this account.

Many airframes will develop a pattern of component cracking and this pattern will be discovered by the manufacturer and reported in maintenance bulletins sent to all authorized repair shops. Good inspectors will know where cracks have been appearing in airplanes of your type and will give an extra close look at those spots.

Unfortunately, there is nothing a pilot can do to prevent airframe cracks beyond reasonable handling of the airplane. Nicks, poor design, or a flaw in the original structure will cause most cracks but some causes are never determined.

Fighting Corrosion

The battle against airframe corrosion is never-ending. Because airplanes are built from lightweight metals, any corrosion can significantly weaken the structure and lead to a failure. It is unlikely that any airplane will fail in flight directly as a result of corrosion damage because the problem can be detected during inspections. But solving a corrosion problem is going to be very expensive unless corrective measures are taken early.

The insidious aspect of corrosion in airframes is that it is most likely to occur in places we can't see. Skin joints, hinges, landing gear attachment points, exhaust areas, and any other hidden structure are common spots for serious corrosion.

Aluminum corrosion will appear as a powder on the surface of unpainted metal. Small pits will develop and the entire corroded area appears rough and dull compared to a noncorroded part. Moisture is the leading cause of corrosion but chemicals, especially electrolytes used in batteries, also lead to corrosion. Unpainted structure is the most common source of corrosion but is also the least difficult to cure. If paint or primer does not bond securely to aluminum, corrosion can attack under the paint and be impossible to detect until serious damage has taken place. Whenever paint blisters on an aircraft, suspect corrosion under the paint.

In light airplanes the fuselage belly will present corrosion problems. For some reason nobody clearly understands, water always finds its way into aircraft bilges or belly areas. Condensation, leaks, and plugged drain holes all contribute to this problem, but whatever the cause you can be sure moisture is collecting in the belly of your airplane.

Oil, dirt, and other forms of crud will join water in the bilge to make a potent corrosive mixture. Fuselage formers, stringers, control cables, and wiring can all be attacked by bilge corrosion and if left unattended can lead to large repair bills.

The solution to corrosion in your airplane's belly is simple to define but difficult to execute—keep the belly clean and dry. All airplanes have drain holes in the underside of wings, tail surfaces, and the fuselage. By keeping these holes open much of the collected moisture can dry out. The next step is to climb back in the fuselage and dig under the floorboards to remove all accumulated dirt. When the metal surface is clean and dry a coating of zinc chromate primer from a spray can will protect the metal until its next cleaning.

Most good inspectors will demand that such a bilge cleaning

take place before approving an annual inspection, but this is a procedure you can do yourself. The only ingredients are hard work and diligence during the cleaning process. When you have your head or entire body back in a tail cone and start spraying zinc chromate primer, be sure you are wearing a paint mask or hold your breath until back out in fresh air. Zinc chromate spray fumes can be very powerful in a small enclosed space and are sure to give you a nasty headache.

Control surfaces are another area to examine for corrosion. Recessed areas where the controls join the airframe are prime corrosion locations because moisture and dirt can collect even though the exterior of the airplane appears clean. Any corrosion you find should be cleaned with medium grit sandpaper and then coated with zinc chromate. Be careful to keep zinc chromate overspray off painted surfaces because it may be difficult to remove.

Be sure to check the underside of wings and tail surfaces closely for surface corrosion. Because moisture clings to these lower surfaces longer and they are hidden from the drying rays of the sun, always expect problems here. Lower wing and tail surface corrosion is so common that when airplanes used to be delivered without paint, they typically were painted on the underside.

There is nothing more appealing than a highly polished aluminum airplane. Virtually all of the Cessna 140s, Luscombes, Swifts, and other classic airplanes of the post-World War II period were delivered with polished metal skins, but few of those airplanes have survived without paint to this day. Bare aluminum skin demands almost constant polishing to keep the dulling effect of corrosion away and most owners have simply given up and painted their airplanes. This surface corrosion was not really a structural problem but did dull the surface. However, unseen corrosion between skin lap joints was a problem on those airplanes and can be a concern on a painted surface.

Most light airplanes are assembled with metal skin pieces overlapping at joints. Moisture can get between the lapped surfaces and cause corrosion that is difficult to detect. Spot-welded lap seams are common corrosion areas because the heat from welding changes the internal structure of the metal alloy. Bubbles or bumps in the surface are about the only evidence of serious corrosion between lap seams. If you see bumps or unevenness appear along a lap seam, suspect corrosion, but it will be up to the IA to decide if the problem is serious enough to demand the joint be disassembled. Good paint can seal lap seams and keep moisture out. If paint cracks and pulls away from lap seams, have it repaired or you may be running the risk of corrosion.

Piano hinges are commonly used to connect control surfaces, cowlings, and other access hatches to an airframe. These hinges are very strong for their weight because the load is distributed over many individual hinge points along the entire length of the hinge. But the fact that these hinges are made of aluminum with a hard steel hinge pin makes corrosion possible because of the effects of dissimilar metals on one another. Also, the small cracks and crevices along a piano hinge are ideal places for moisture and dirt to collect.

Piano hinges must be kept clean and dry but must also be lubricated for smooth operation. Lubricating a hinge with conventional oil or grease is a mistake because the oily surface will attract dirt and dust, which then can hold moisture. The solution is to clean the hinge and spray it with a penetrating lubricant spray that displaces moisture but leaves a very light lubricating film. These spray lubes are available under many brand names, so just look for one that claims to penetrate, lubricate, and displace moisture.

Control Surface Maintenance Problems

Every annual inspection will include a very close look at the control system and lubrication of all moving parts. Light airplane controls are purely mechanical combinations of chains, sprockets, pushrods, bell cranks, cables, and pulleys, which wear, become loose, and can break.

Most light airplane control systems begin with bicycle-type chains and sprocket wheels connecting the two control wheels to central cables. The control wheels are mounted on a main framework behind the panel, which transfers in-out wheel motion to elevator cable movement. These cables will usually join rudder cables under the floor and proceed through pulley networks to the various control surfaces. At the control surface a bell crank transforms the cable motion into the necessary push-pull motion to move the controls. Rudder cables may simply attach to a control horn and elevator cables often attach to a control horn on the spar carry-through.

The point is, when an IA examines this maze of control workings it is not unusual for him to find something wrong. The most common problem is incorrect cable tension which induces slop in the flight controls and in an extreme case could lead to flutter of the control surface. Light airplane control cable tension is not extremely critical but your airplane cannot fly its best without correct tension.

Cable tension is changed by adjusting turnbuckles located somewhere along the cable run. The turnbuckle simply changes the length of the cable and is tightened to add cable tension. Tension is measured by a special tool that clamps over the cable and gauges the amount of pressure needed to deflect the cable. Most inspectors will not measure cable tension unless something looks wrong or the pilot complains of flight control problems when the aircraft comes in for the annual.

Another common control problem is chafe. If a cable is too loose or if some object is allowed to rub against control cables, chafe can soon wear the cable and weaken its rated strength. Aircraft control cable is made of twisted wire strands and if any of the strands are worn by chafe, the cable must be replaced.

Corrosion also attacks control cables, especially if they lay in bilge water for any period. Stainless steel control cables are available as an option on some new aircraft, especially for use in seaplanes, but most airplanes do not have stainless cables. If corrosion is suspected in a cable, the mechanic will loosen its tension and twist the cable against its normal twist, forcing the strands apart so he can see if any corrosion is present between strands. Again, the only solution for this problem is replacing the cable.

The adjustment of flight control surfaces is called rig and during an inspection the IA will always look at the rig of an airplane. An out-of-rig airplane may have one aileron too high or improper travel in the elevator or other problems. The airplane manufacturer establishes precise rig settings and the mechanic can use these specifications to rerig an airplane by adjusting the turnbuckles. An airplane can fall out of proper rig because of wear or stretch in the cables, pulleys, or other control system components.

Wear and resultant slop in control hinges and control pushrod ends is a very common problem in light airplanes. Wear in these areas allows control surfaces to vibrate during flight, which accelerates wear further. Some slop will always be present in any control system but it takes an expert mechanic to know when normal slop limits have been exceeded and a problem exists. As pilots we should always wiggle control surfaces with our hands during preflight inspection to see if large amounts of slop are present. If you think there is a problem, ask a mechanic to check.

The best way to fight control slop and wear as an airplane owner is to lubricate control hinges and control cable or pushrod bearings regularly. Do not use heavy oils or grease that will attract dirt. Your owner's handbook should provide a list of recommended lubricants for each job.

Landing Gear Problems

Landing gear, whether fixed or retractable, are going to be a source of problems on any airframe. Even the best pilot bounces a landing now and then, placing the gear under extreme loads. But the real problems are caused by wear and corrosion.

Many parts of a landing gear must be made from steel to have enough strength to hold up to landing shock. Steel is, as we all know, very prone to rust. The landing gear spends all its time working down in the water and dirt of the runway and any corrosion problems will be accelerated by these conditions. Keeping your landing gear clean and painted is the best way to prevent corrosion.

Retractable landing gear have many moving parts which wear and corrode. Grease fittings should be lubricated on the recommended schedule and the gear should be kept clean and free of dirt. Wheel wells are a particularly nasty corrosion problem because the tires throw water and mud up in the wells during takeoff or landing and the dirt will stay there unless somebody washes it out. Most wheel wells have seams and lap edges that catch and hold dirt and water and on a twin, engine exhaust also blasts both the gear and wells.

As every taildragger owner knows, tail wheels are constant problems. Because most tail wheels are so small they turn at very high rpm during takeoff and landing rolls. Any unbalance or slop in the tail wheel will show up as severe vibration. The fuselage tail cone of a metal taildragger is shaped just like a megaphone with you sitting at the amplified end, so any tail wheel problems will translate into some very loud and bothersome sounds during ground operation.

Most tail wheel problems can be traced to slop in wheel bearings or the swivel bearing of the tail wheel itself. Because a tail wheel is so small it is often under water or at least up to its bearings in water when parked on a wet ramp or, worse yet, when parked in wet grass. Moisture causes corrosion, which leads to accelerated wear and slop. The solution is to keep the tail wheel as dry as possible by propping it up out of standing water if you can and by keeping everything on the tail wheel assembly well greased.

Almost certain tail wheel problems will occur with this tail wheel resting in thick grass. Moisture will invade the wheel bearings, which can quickly cause vibration and wear to the tail wheel swivel bearing. The solution is to keep tail wheels propped up out of grass and water and keep the wheels greased.

Is Hangaring Worth the Money?

Moisture and sunlight are two of the most destructive forces working against an airplane. Moisture promotes corrosion and sunlight accelerates deterioration of paint, fabric, rubber, and plexiglass. The combined results are that an airplane parked outside will require more maintenance than one stored in a hangar. The question is will it cost more to pay hangar rents or pay increased maintenance bills?

There are no easy or absolute answers to those questions but I can discuss some of the many variables that will help you decide.

A major factor in the hangaring decision is how long you plan to keep your airplane. An airplane in good condition can be stored outside for a couple of years and show no serious ill effects that will detract from its resale value. If you sell it quickly, the early problems of moisture and sunlight will belong to somebody else. But if you plan to keep your airplane, a hangar can save enough in paint, interior, tire, and window damage nearly to pay for itself.

If your airplane is covered with fabric rather than metal, hangaring is essential. All fabric coverings are painted with a silver undercoat to help protect against the sun's ultraviolet rays but these rays will still damage the covering. Man-made coverings such as Dacron will last much longer than grade A cotton but the sun will even take years off the lives of these materials. Sunlight damages all types of paint but is especially harmful to dope used on fabric cover because it makes the dope brittle. Brittle dope will develop tiny hairline cracks and if struck by your fist or some other blunt object will show what is called a bird's nest of concentric rings of cracks in the paint. Moisture and more sunlight can enter these cracks and further damage the covering below. Dried and brittle dope can be helped by something called rejuvenator, a very strong paint thinner which is applied to old dope surfaces. The rejuvenator softens the dope and helps fill cracks to get a few more years of use out of an old dope finish.

The climate in which you live is also important in the hangaring decision. Cold northern winters are inconvenient and it is

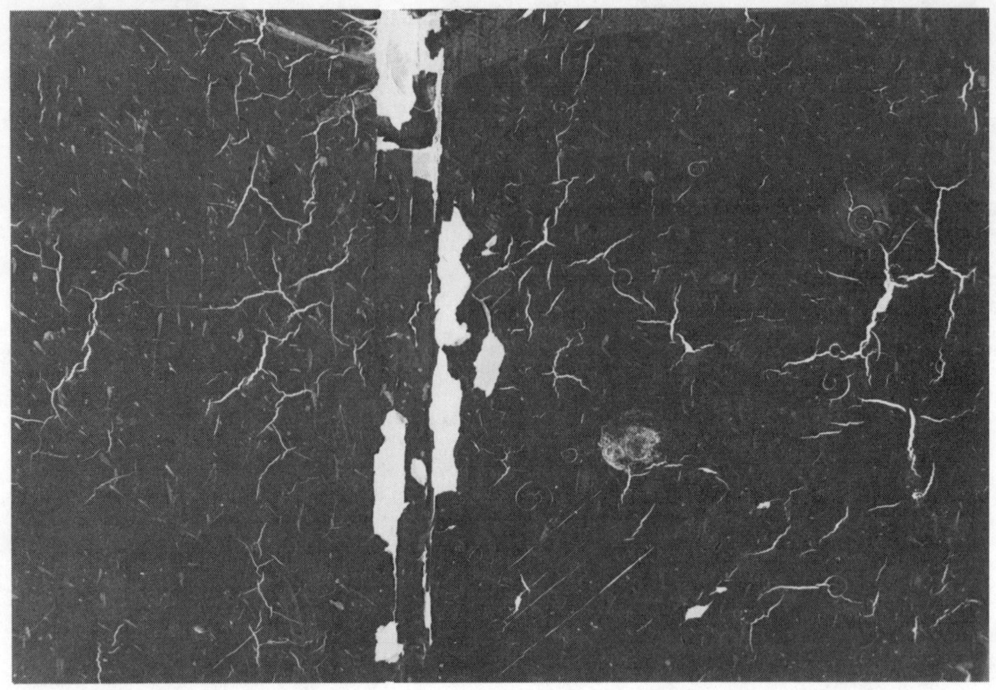

The dope paint finish on this fabric-covered wing has been badly damaged by the sun. These cracks, called ringworm, allow sun and moisture to enter below the dope coating and rot the fabric cover. Protection from sunlight is the best preventive measure you can take for fabric-covered airplanes.

difficult to remove snow and ice before takeoff but the permanent damage done to your airplane is less than if it is exposed to very hot sun in the Southwest.

Perhaps the real clincher in any decision about renting a hangar is how you feel about your airplane. If you don't care how it looks and don't care if the paint is oxidized and the interior faded, a hangar probably won't be worth the money to you. But even if you don't mind flying a faded airplane with rotting rubber seals and bleached-out seats, others do and the value of your airplane at resale time will be considerably less.

7

Avionics and How to Keep Them Working and Make a Coherent Installation

For many private pilots avionics, the official term for all types of airplane radios, have become nearly as important as the engine or airframe. The air traffic control system covers so much airspace that it is impossible to use our airplanes without proper electronic equipment. A friend of mine who flew his Cessna 182 extensively out of the New York City area had two transponders and encoding altimeters installed because he worried more about losing ATC contact than losing his engine.

The average new single-engine retractable airplane will have nearly $20,000 worth of avionics installed and some sophisticated singles like the Cessna 210s, Bonanzas, and Mooneys will have more than $30,000 worth of avionics. Flight control systems, weather radar, RNAV, and nearly every other system that is available in business jets or airliners is available to the light airplane owner.

If you are trying to determine the age of a popular airplane like a Bonanza or Cessna 182, it may be difficult unless you can see the panel. There has been little change in airplanes and engines over the past ten years, but avionics have gone through a revolution. Those of us who fly heavy IFR in single-engine airplanes take DME, good autopilots, and reliable navcoms for granted in new airplanes. Without this equipment airplanes are limited to VFR and that only in uncrowded airspace away from the TCAs, which cover virtually all major cities.

The avionics package in this Bonanza is typical of the well-equipped sophisticated single. Dual navs, coms, DME, transponder, ADF, and flight control systems all help make the modern single-engine airplane a useful IFR machine.

My point is that airplane radios are not a luxury anymore. If you can't keep the avionics working, the airplane will not be of much use no matter how good the airframe and engine are.

All avionics maintenance, except for the transponder and encoder, is on condition. That means there are no inspection or service requirements for radios and the best advice from experts is that if your equipment appears to be working, leave it alone. There are no tune-ups, or checkups, or any other type of regular maintenance that can help your equipment until it breaks. But there are some techniques we can all use to increase the odds that our avionics will live long useful lives.

The most common avionics killers are heat and moisture. Heat is generated inside all radios as electrical power is dissipated through various electronic components. Electrical power cannot simply vanish but must be transformed into some other type of energy. Most electrical power used in radios is converted to heat as it performs its function flowing through resistors, capacitors, transistors, and other devices. Removing this heat and keeping the radios cool is vital.

Modern transistorized radios use very little electrical power compared to earlier tube-type avionics, therefore less heat is generated. The "Catch 22" in this development is that although less total heat is created by new radios, more components and capability are packed in a smaller box than tube-type radios, making heat more difficult to dissipate. The change to solid-state transistor components reduced the total heat problem but concentrated remaining heat in smaller boxes where it can do the most damage.

Most of the responsibility for solving avionics heat problems belongs to the equipment installer. Cooling air flow is required and usually comes from a ram air scoop on the forward side of the fuselage. If you'll look at your airplane between the door and

This scoop draws in ram cooling air for avionics. The scoop should be kept free of dirt and insects and if your airplane doesn't have such a scoop, you should consult an avionics shop to be certain your airplane has adequate avionics cooling.

nose, you should find a small air scoop. This scoop is connected to a plastic hose which runs to the radio stack where air flows into a diffuser to spread the flow across all radios in the stack. If this type of ram air is not supplied to your radios, you can expect problems. Some avionics manufacturers will even void warranties if proper ram cooling air is not supplied.

In the Bonanza I now fly, somebody forgot to hook up the cooling air hose leading to the horizontal gyro which drives the HSI. For nearly two years the gyro performed well and nobody knew that it wasn't receiving cooling air until it failed. The gyro should have lasted longer than it did and probably would have had that cooling air been provided.

If you are buying a new avionics package or even a single radio, be certain to discuss cooling with the shop. If you have purchased a used airplane, it is worth the money to take the airplane to a good avionics shop and have the radio installation inspected for adequate cooling. If the original installer cut corners on cooling, have more cooling equipment added. It will save you money later.

Heat can also be a problem when the airplane is sitting on a hot sunny ramp. The greenhouse effect of the windshield can elevate temperatures under the aircraft instrument panel to 150 degrees F. or more, damaging radios even though they are not turned on. When you turn the radios on under these conditions, and power flows through very hot components, any weak spots in the circuit will fail.

One obvious way to avoid overheating avionics when the airplane is at rest is to store it in a hangar. When that is not possible the next best cooling method is to use sunscreens in the windshield. The best screens are bright silver-colored cloth which can reflect nearly all of the sun's heat. Several companies offer custom-made sunscreens which fit in the windshield and windows and are held in place by Velcro tabs. I recommend the fitted screens if you store your airplane outside continuously because they will protect both the avionics and interior from sun damage. If you keep your airplane in a hangar at home base, I think a silver-colored blanket commonly sold as a beach blanket will do the job. Simply drape the blanket over the instrument panel glare shield and front seats and you will have adequate

The sunscreens installed in this airplane reflect sun rays, keeping avionics cool and protecting the interior from fading. Sunscreens can lower cabin temperatures by more than 50 degrees on a hot, sunny ramp.

protection for those times when your airplane must sit out away from home.

The second common avionics killer is moisture entering the radios. Airplane windshields leak and if your airplane sits outside all the time, water will probably find its way into the radios. I can remember going on a demonstration in a brand-new Piper Aztec with a salesman showing me a sophisticated avionics package. After about 15 minutes of flying, the combined navcom-audio panel started to smoke heavily and we had to pull circuit breakers to put out the fire. When the radio was removed from the panel, water ran out, explaining exactly why we had the failure—the windshield had leaked during a thunderstorm the night before.

Again, hangaring your airplane is the best way to keep the avionics dry. If that is not possible, maintain a close watch on

Exterior window covers such as this protect avionics and interior from sun heat and also help stop rain water from leaking into avionics. In the winter exterior covers can be quickly removed, leaving a frost-free windshield beneath.

windshield seals. Make certain the rubber has not dried out or the caulking pulled away. Some windshield leaks simply are impossible to solve, especially in older airplanes, and in that situation I recommend one of the many outside canvas windshield covers that are available. These covers will keep moisture and sun out and in the winter will keep frost off the windshield.

Another moisture-fighting technique is to keep all of your radios turned on while flying. Modern solid-state avionics do not have wear-out components that fail in direct proportion to use so there is nothing to be gained by turning off radios when you are not using them in flight. Instead, by keeping your avionics power turned on, the radios will operate at normal temperatures, drying out any moisture that may have condensed inside the boxes since the last use. Also, any electronic equipment is most likely to fail when it is turned on and off. If you turn on all radios at the start of each flight and leave them on, they are less likely to fail during that flight than if you are constantly turning them off and on as you use them.

Reporting an Avionics Failure

One of the best ways to save money on avionics repair is to make a thorough and accurate failure report to the shop. If you tell the avionics shop nothing more than that a radio doesn't work, you will pay for all the time they spend troubleshooting to determine how and when it doesn't operate.

When you have an avionics problem be as observant as possible. Note what frequency or frequencies the radio is tuned to when problems occur. Check circuit breakers, audio control switches, and even something as simple as the on-off knobs. I remember one flight where I spent an hour mentally cursing noise in my com radios before discovering that I had accidentally bumped the audio switch for the DME. What I was hearing was the DME squitter, not noise from my coms.

Before you blame your avionics, remember that most equipment is simply receiving signals from the ground. Those outside signals may be to blame rather than your avionics. On many flights I have had controllers tell me my transponder or encoding altimeter was not working but the next center or approach sector had no problem receiving my transponder signal. Was my transponder failing intermittently? No, it was simply a problem of ground equipment not working properly or something on the ground or airplane blocking the path between my transponder antenna and the ground radar site. One pattern I did finally identify was that controllers would always lose my transponder when I was being vectored directly to the airport and in a steep descent. When I noticed this pattern of radar contact loss I checked my transponder antenna location and sure enough, it was on the fuselage belly directly behind the nose gear. When I lowered the nose to descend it blocked the path between the transponder and ground antennas.

Total failures are the easiest to identify and are usually the quickest to repair. If a nav receiver simply will not receive any ground station, that is all you need report to the avionics shop.

The problem must be in the receiver or antenna and the shop can quickly determine which is the problem by bench-testing the receiver.

Intermittent failures are another matter. They are difficult to identify, report, and repair. The frustrating thing about intermittent failures is that neither you nor the shop knows when the problem has been licked until something positively broken can be identified.

We recently had a frustrating intermittent problem with the autopilot in our Bonanza. For no apparent reason the autopilot would automatically disengage. The first repair shop I took the airplane to concluded the problem was in the wheel-mounted trim switch, which was giving false commands to the autopilot. They replaced the switch at a cost of several hundred dollars and the problem continued.

Finally, after flying with this problem for nearly 100 hours I noticed that the autopilot would never disengage in either basic autopilot or altitude hold mode. Because I always fly in heading hold mode I hadn't noticed that it would not disengage without heading mode engaged. With this information the shop knew the problem was in the heading channel, not the pitch channel, and most likely was an invalid signal from the directional gyro. Sure enough, that was the problem. The directional gyro was sending a false signal to the autopilot saying the gyro had failed. After two abortive trips to the shop and several hundred dollars in unnecessary repairs, the problem was located because I was lucky and observant, not because the shop was super sharp.

I have found that intermittent failures must be observed for several flights before you can learn enough to make an accurate and helpful report to the repair shop. Try to note every circumstance surrounding the intermittent failure when it occurs. For example, how long has the radio been turned on? Are you flying in rain or dry air? Have you flown through severe bumps before it quits? What is the outside air temperature? What frequency or frequencies does it quit on? Try to establish a pattern for the failures even if you think the circumstances have nothing to do with the radio.

When you have learned all you can about a failure, never pull the radios from the airplane and take them to the shop yourself. Nearly half of all failures will be installation-related, that is the problem is in wires or antennas in the airplane, not with the radio itself. If you take only the suspect radio to the shop for work, there is a fifty-fifty chance that you are taking the wrong equipment to the shop and time and money will be wasted in the eventual repair.

Most avionics shops sell and repair all major brands so it is not as difficult to select a radio repair shop as it is to find a shop for your airplane. Avionics manufacturers publish service bulletins and your shop should have a complete file covering all avionics it repairs. If the shop does not have current service publications, go somewhere else because many failures will be covered by service bulletins.

When your avionics equipment is in for repair, ask the shop staff to research service bulletins published for your equipment. Discuss each bulletin outstanding against your equipment to determine if it is worth having these bulletin modifications performed on your radio while it is in the shop. If your shop foreman says that a bulletin covers a common problem but your radio does not have that problem, it may be worth the money to have the bulletin complied with to prevent a future failure. Only a knowledgeable shop foreman can explain the cost versus benefits of service bulletins, but in many cases it will be less costly to have modifications performed before a failure takes place than to send the radio back to the shop and suffer additional aircraft downtime.

Building an Avionics System

The more sophisticated our avionics become, the more each individual box depends on other elements of the avionics system. The more of this type of avionics integration that takes place, the more planning we must do to be certain that future elements of the system will fit in.

For example, when you select a basic navcom package, make certain the nav receiver outputs are compatible with an HSI (Horizontal Situation Indicator) should you wish to add that instrument in the future. Another example is integration of an RNAV with your DME and nav receivers. Not all RNAVs can work with all DMEs or nav receivers.

One way to plan your panel is to stick entirely with one single brand of avionics. Every manufacturer assures the buyer that all elements of its product line will play together. The drawback of this approach is that other manufacturers may offer better products in a specific area and you may not be able to use that product.

I believe a more logical approach to avionics buying decisions is to develop a long range plan. Decide what equipment you eventually plan to have in the airplane and make early decisions based on the total system. Get together with an avionics shop foreman, discuss your ultimate plan, and decide exactly what types of equipment you can afford and will work best in your airplane.

If you are buying a new airplane, the place to start avionics

HSIs such as this King KCS-55A are popular in light airplanes but if you plan to install an HSI or other advanced equipment later, be certain avionics you buy now are compatible with future equipment.

planning is with the flight control system. Autopilots are the most difficult type of avionics to add to older airplanes. It is just as difficult and expensive to replace a cheap, low-capability autopilot with a new one later, so select the best possible autopilot when you specify your new avionics package.

Autopilots must be specifically approved for each model of airplane they are installed in. It is not possible to get any autopilot in any airplane because manufacturers only certified their autopilots in airplanes they anticipated would be prime prospects. If you want a very expensive autopilot in an inexpensive airplane, it may not be possible.

There is a great deal of controversy over who should install avionics—the airplane manufacturer or an avionics shop—and there are pluses for both sides. But I believe that no matter where you decide to have your avionics installed you should have the autopilot installed by the airplane manufacturer if at all possible. Autopilots require installation of servo motors on the controls and several other steps that usually result in considerable disassembly of an airplane. If the autopilot is installed at the airplane factory, all of these elements are in place before the interior and other final components are installed, making a cleaner and neater installation. It is possible for an avionics shop to do just as good a job of installing an autopilot, but it will probably be more costly and means your airplane must be torn apart and reassembled in the process.

If you decide to have the airplane manufacturer install other avionics, you will get a good installation and the airplane will be ready to fly as soon as you get it. The manufacturer will be able to install antennas and wires before the airplane is complete for a tidy job. I have seen many excellent factory avionics installations, especially from Beech, but I have also flown a few airplanes with terrible factory avionics work. If you get a poor factory installation, then you have to fight it out with the airplane dealer to get service and he may not have adequate avionics capability to solve your problems.

On the other hand, if you have an independent radio shop install your avionics, you have total freedom to select any avionics package you wish and also have somebody standing behind the work. Shop-installed avionics may cost a little less

These radios have been installed by Beechcraft, the label says, and Beech has done an excellent job. The decision between factory-installed avionics and field installations is a difficult one to make, but the factory installation wins if time is a consideration.

than similar equipment installed at the airplane factory, but your airplane may be unusable for a couple of weeks or longer while the avionics are installed.

Cost will probably balance out between shop- and factory-installed avionics, leaving you to decide between the convenience of a fully equipped airplane the day you pick it up and the custom installation and support of an independent shop. My feeling is that if you have a good avionics shop near your home airport, buy from them. If you do not have positive feelings about any radio shop near you, I would elect the factory-installed avionics and get the equipment repaired at whatever shop is convenient.

Owners of older airplanes should consider buying used avionics when they need additional capability. Most shops accept avionics in trade for new equipment and usually have a good supply of used equipment on hand. Trade-ins are tested and any defects repaired before they are sold and most shops will offer a sixty or ninety-day warranty on the equipment.

There is nothing for the prospective used avionics customer to fear except lack of integrity by the shop he or she is dealing with. New avionics carry a one-year warranty that you will not get with a used box, but the used equipment has been in service and has had time to be debugged.

I would not recommend buying used avionics that are more than one generation old, not because it is not good equipment, but because service personnel will not have recent experience working on it. For example, King Radio now has a new line of Silver Crown equipment that is excellent but there are thousands of KX 170 and KX 175 navcoms around that are the most popular navcoms ever built and are excellent used selections. However, KX 170 and KX 175 navcoms are now two generations old and few shops will have had any recent experience with that navcom, making repair more expensive.

Be careful when buying any used transponder. There have been several changes in transponder specifications in the past and early units that did not meet current TSO specs were outlawed. There may still be some of these worthless boxes around and an unscrupulous shop may pass those transponders off on a used avionics customer.

Airworthiness Directives and How to Deal With Them

Airworthiness Directives, AD Notes as they are normally known, lurk in the worst nightmares of all airplane owners. An AD Note can pop up at any time demanding extensive aircraft repair or modification at very great expense. There is nothing we as airplane owners can do to prevent ADs except hope they are not issued for our airplanes.

Although ADs can be painful to our budgets they are necessary. Every AD is issued to correct a serious safety problem and they are only issued after significant evidence has been compiled. Once an airplane defect has been identified and the FAA has determined that a safety hazard exists, the AD Note defines corrective action. All ADs carry the force of law and must be complied with or an affected airplane is legally unairworthy.

AD Notes can trace their roots to the earliest days of aviation in the United States. Early federal air inspectors would note maintenance problems during aircraft inspections and issue "maintenance notes" when serious problems were uncovered. In the period after World War II the Civil Aeronautics Authority, predecessor of the FAA, renamed maintenance notes AD Notes and developed a process for issuing and enforcing the new directives.

The first step, and certainly the most difficult part of the procedure of developing an AD, is determining when safety-related problems exist. As you may guess, crashes are a common source of ADs, but there are several other ways defects can be identified.

All airplane crashes are analyzed by the FAA and fatal crashes are analyzed by the National Transportation Safety Board (NTSB). The NTSB has sole authority to determine the cause of any crash and does so in every fatal incident but the FAA examines all crashes for possible aircraft defects.

Most crashes are the result of pilot mistakes and in no way can be blamed on the airplane. But in that minority of accidents where something on the airplane failed, the FAA and NTSB will go to extreme lengths to find out what went wrong. One recent example of an airframe failure leading to an accident was the Cessna Conquest tail failure and crash in 1977. The NTSB determined the crash was caused by an elevator trim tab failure and the FAA issued an emergency AD grounding all Conquest aircraft until the trim tab could be modified.

However, most airframe or mechanical failures leading to crashes do not result in AD Notes. If the failure was caused by poor maintenance, a mistake in aircraft manufacture, or abuse, no AD will be issued because other aircraft of the same type should not have the same problem. Before an AD is issued it must be determined that the structural failure was caused by a faulty design or normal wear.

When airplanes grow old and accumulate thousands of operational hours problems that were never anticipated during original design and construction may show up. For example, the venerable Beech 18 became the subject of several AD Notes against its wing spar after many years of service. The original spar design was sound but engineers did not correctly predict the impact of long service life.

Air crashes are the most spectacular result of a pilot or aircraft failure and both the FAA and NTSB are under public pressure to prevent recurrence. However, the NTSB cannot and will not issue AD Notes. It will make recommendations to the FAA but it is up to that agency to determine if a true safety hazard does exist. The FAA will also consider whether there is a reasonable solution and will attempt to determine what percentage of the aircraft fleet suffers from the problem before issuing an AD.

Another means of identifying a safety hazard is through the Malfunction and Defect Report all maintenance shops are required to file with the FAA when they encounter an unusual problem. Normal wear and tear will not be reported but if a mechanic spots a serious problem, such as cracks in key structural areas or other unexplained failures, he will make a report. Pilots are also encouraged to make reports of unusual problems or aircraft failures in flight. If you think a problem is serious, call your local FAA General Aviation District Office (GADO) so that corrective action can begin immediately.

Reports from the field may provide enough information for the FAA to proceed with an AD but in many cases a fact-finding AD may be issued. These fact-finding ADs must be complied with like any other AD but normally only require an inspection and report. If most aircraft do not have the reported defect, the AD Note will be withdrawn. If inspections reveal that many subject airplanes do have a problem, a final fix will be determined and a new AD issued describing that procedure.

Aircraft manufacturers are another common source of information leading to AD Notes. The manufacturers normally learn of serious problems because shops will call to get information on how to repair unusual defects. If the defect presents a serious

The Malfunction and Defect Report is required when any unusual aircraft mechanical failure is discovered. Mechanics normally fill out these reports but pilots are also encouraged to make reports if they discover a serious safety problem. All Malfunction and Defect Reports are analyzed by the FAA and may result in an AD Note to correct the problem.

1. REGISTRATION NO.
N–

DEPARTMENT OF TRANSPORTATION
FEDERAL AVIATION ADMINISTRATION
MALFUNCTION OR DEFECT REPORT

Form Approved Budget Bureau No. 04–R0003

8. DATE SUB.

FOR FAA USE ONLY
CONTROL NO.

	A. MAKE	B. MODEL	C. SERIAL NO.
2. AIRCRAFT			
3. POWERPLANT			
4. PROPELLER			

5. APPLIANCE/COMPONENT (*assy. that includes part*)

A. NAME	B. MAKE	C. MODEL	D. SERIAL NO.

6. SPECIFIC PART (*of component*) CAUSING TROUBLE

A. NAME	B. NUMBER	C. PART/DEFECT LOCATION

FAA USE D. ATA CODE	E. PART TT	F. PART TSO	G. PART CONDITION

7A. COMMENTS (*Describe the malfunction or defect and the circumstances under which it occurred. State probable cause and recommendations to prevent recurrence.*)

Continue on reverse

SUBMITTED BY

B.	C.	D.	E.	F.	G.	H.	I.
REP. STA.	OPER.	MECH.	AIR TAXI	MFG.	FAA	OTHER	

FAA FORM 8330–2 (6-75) SUPERSEDES PREVIOUS EDITIONS

safety problem, the manufacturer will notify the FAA and discuss the possible issuance of an AD. In any case, the manufacturer will develop and publish a service bulletin describing how a specific problem should be repaired.

You may believe airplane manufacturers would attempt to avoid ADs or issuing information that might lead to an AD and at one time that was the situation. However, product liability risks are so great manufacturers now welcome ADs in many instances because an AD forces all owners to repair a defect. Without an AD an owner may neglect to have a problem corrected and any crash resulting from that problem could put the manufacturer in tenuous legal liability straits. But when an AD is issued the airplane owner is responsible for making certain the AD is complied with.

Once a defect has been identified and it is found to exist in a significant number of airplanes, the FAA must determine how to correct the problem. Typically engineers from the FAA will meet with engineers from the airplane manufacturer and develop a solution. In every situation the FAA will attempt to keep the corrective action as minimal as possible. Many ADs will require nothing more than repetitive inspections. Most ADs will have some operational time limit for compliances, allowing operators to take their airplanes to a shop at their convenience. For example, an AD may require inspection and repair within the next 25 flight hours.

In extreme situations the FAA will issue an emergency AD, which requires a specific inspection or repair before further flight. The emergency AD has no operational time cushion, so it effectively grounds the fleet until inspections or repairs can be made. Emergency ADs are not the norm but there have been some affecting light airplanes. For example, a bad batch of oil coolers were installed in some Cessna singles and Mooneys and an emergency AD grounded those airplanes until new oil coolers were installed. If the oil coolers had failed in flight, engine oil would have been lost, stopping the engine and leading to an almost certain accident.

All ADs, because they become part of U.S. aviation law, are published in the Federal Register. The Federal Register is some of the dullest reading you can ever encounter so few airplane

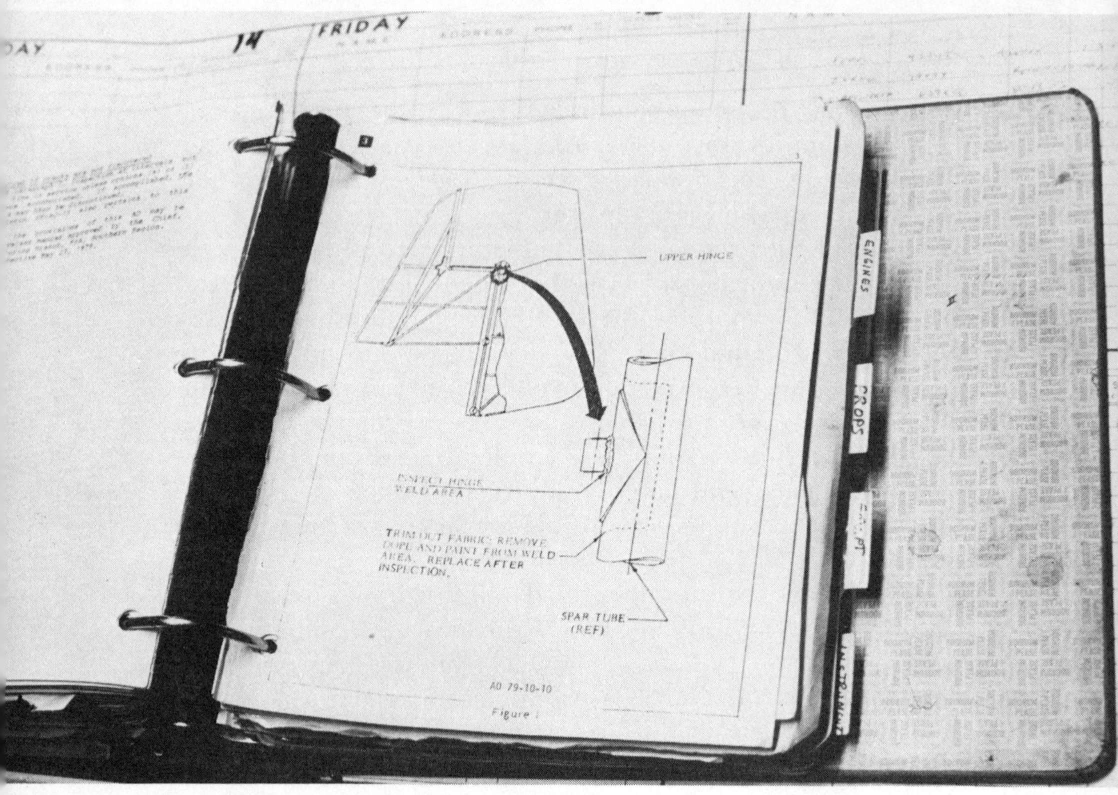

Some AD Notes, such as the one shown here, contain diagrams directing inspection and repair but most are nothing more than a written description of the required repair or inspection.

owners ever see an AD published there. Most owners will be notified of an AD through the mail, based on FAA aircraft ownership records stored in Oklahoma City. Emergency ADs are normally telegraphed to registered owners, warning them not to fly their airplanes.

FAA ownership records are computerized and one would think very sophisticated, but that is not the case. After I sold my last airplane the FAA sent me registration forms, believing I was still the owner, for the next two years. Also, the FAA stores the official ownership address, which may be a leasing company, bank, or corporate headquarters. AD Notes mailed to those addresses may never reach the airplane operator who is supposed to take the airplane to the shop. However, because you do not receive an AD Note in the mail you are not off the hook for compliance, so I recommend that you keep a good relationship with your maintenance shop foreman because he will receive ADs and can notify you.

AD Notes are not as precise and clear cut as you may imagine. For example, we recently received an AD Note for magnetos on our company Bonanza. The problem mags were installed in several engine models but the FAA did not know which engines or even which airplanes had the defective mag. So all airplanes that used the engines which may have had the defective mags got the AD in the mail. Our shop foreman simply looked under the cowl, determined we had a totally different brand of mags, and that was the end of compliance with that AD.

Paying for AD required work is a sore point with all airplane owners but there is some relief in sight. All manufacturers will pay for parts and labor necessary to comply with an AD during new aircraft warranty periods and many times will pick up the cost on airplanes out of warranty. If your airplane is reasonably new, always go to a certified dealer if an AD is issued for your airplane. If the manufacturer is going to pay for any or all of the cost of an AD, it will pay only if its dealers do the work.

There have been legislative proposals at the state level which would require aircraft manufacturers to pay the total cost of any AD no matter the age of the aircraft. It is doubtful these state laws could ever be effective because airplanes are regulated by the federal government. However, pressure is growing for manufacturers to pay for ADs because all ADs represent at least a small error in judgment during initial aircraft design.

You would think that aircraft design has improved over the years and we should see fewer ADs but that is not happening. In fact, the total number of ADs issued has increased in the past ten years and many of those notices have been directed at new design airplanes. One possible explanation is that new construction materials and methods are being used and may not prove satisfactory in actual service. Another reason for the increase in ADs is that both the FAA and manufacturers fear liability suits that are sure to result from any inflight structural failure.

When you consider buying a used airplane, the AD history of that particular model and the way in which the ADs have been complied with on the specific airplane you are considering are very important. You may change your mind about that model of airplane if there are many complex ADs issued for it.

To review an airplane model's AD history you can visit an FAA/GADO (General Aviation District Office), which usually maintains a record of all ADs issued against general aviation aircraft. However, the official FAA version of an AD can be difficult to read because of the obtuse wording favored by all federal agencies. Instead of going to a GADO I recommend you visit a maintenance shop that specializes in the type of airplane you are interested in. The shop foreman will know and have on record all ADs outstanding against airplanes he commonly inspects. It will be worth your money to pay that shop manager, usually an IA, for his time both to research the AD history and inspect the airplane you are thinking of buying. There are also several publishing companies that offer an AD research service tailored to

A summary of AD Notes for light airplanes fills this fat notebook. Any good shop will have this book on hand and will refer to the summary during inspections to be certain all ADs are complied with.

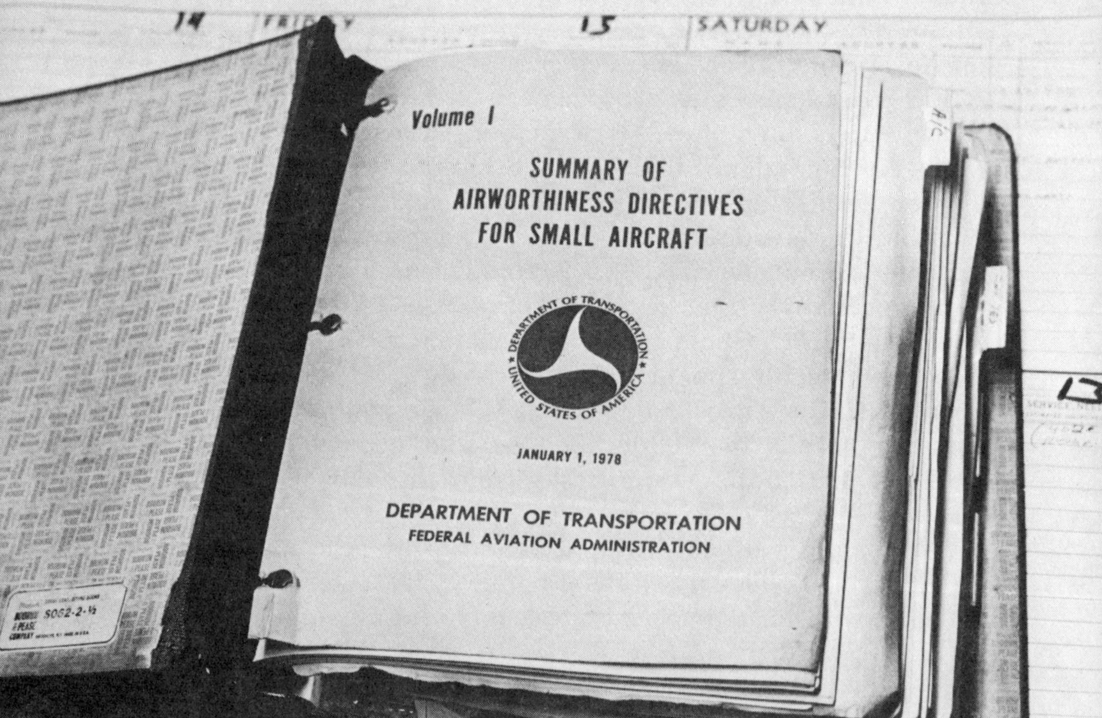

specific aircraft models. You can find listings of these companies in aviation directory publications.

Once you have determined which ADs have been issued against the model airplane you are considering, the next step is to find out how those ADs have been complied with. It is common procedure for aircraft logbooks to carry the entry "all ADs complied with" after an annual inspection record. This sounds encouraging and may mean there are no ADs outstanding. However, many ADs offer a choice of repeated inspections at specific operational time intervals or replacement of the defective part. An AD has been complied with if the inspections take place, but if you are buying a used airplane you want the defective part to be replaced, not merely inspected.

Only a thorough search of an aircraft's records can establish exactly how and if ADs have been complied with. Again, it will be difficult for an unknowledgeable person to gain all the answers from maintenance logs and records. Pay an IA to examine all records before you purchase an airplane. If records are incomplete or missing, beware. You may still decide to buy an airplane with poor maintenance records but don't pay top dollar because good records are a reason one airplane is worth more than another.

Sometimes AD Notes are of such latitude that you can operate the airplane for years before actual compliance must take place. For example, an AD was issued against the magnetos on an airplane I once owned, requiring replacement of the mags within 200 hours. That amount of flight time represented well over a year of flying for me so I kept the airplane until the 200 hours had nearly expired and sold it. The notation in the logs said all ADs were complied with and they were. I do not know if the new owner investigated the AD situation but he should have.

9

Safe and Saving Operating Techniques:

The Best Way to Save on Maintenance Bills

Probably the best way to save money on aircraft maintenance is to operate the airplane in such a way that its life is extended to the fullest. We can never avoid the many required inspections or regular preventive maintenance costs but safe and saving operational techniques can extract more useful flight hours from any airplane.

As I have stated many times in this book, the engine on any airplane represents the single greatest maintenance expense. Fortunately, the engine is also the easiest airplane element to protect through good operating practices.

Every pilot knows that reducing power in cruise can save both fuel and engine wear, but sound engine operating practice begins long before you reach cruise flight. It begins even before engine start.

Lubricating oil is the lifeblood of any engine and any oil system neglect will lead to excessive wear. Engine oil must be changed at recommended intervals and must be of the weight and type specified by the manufacturer. If an oil weight heavier than recommended is used, it will be too thick to flow properly during engine start and warm-up. Engineers calculate that more than half of all engine wear takes place in the first minutes of operation after each start because oil is thick and does not lubricate properly.

Air temperature is the most important determining factor in

oil weight selection. Most modern engines will use 50 weight SAE aircraft oil under normal summer temperatures with a change to 40 weight if average temperatures drop below 70 degrees F. and another change to 30 weight for normal winter operations. When temperatures are below freezing even 30 weight oil becomes thick and flows slowly, so engine preheat is required.

We have all seen engine preheat operations on a cold morning at the airport but many times the procedure is incorrect and inadequate. Heated air can be directed over the cylinders and the engine will warm up and start quickly. However, this is not solving the really damaging problem of cold, thick oil. Preheat should be directed primarily at the oil sump and oil cooler to warm and thin oil so that it can flow through the engine immedi-

The yellow line at the 40 degrees C. position on this Bonanza oil temperature gauge indicates the engine should not be run at high speed until oil temperature has reached that level. Until oil is at least that warm it cannot properly flow through the engine to lubricate all working parts and even a run-up with cold oil can cause damage.

ately after start-up. If engine preheat air is being forced in over the cylinders, plug air exit vents under the cowling so the warm air will be forced down to the lower sections of the engine where the oil is stored.

Under extremely cold temperatures—near zero or below—oil can actually coagulate into a semisolid mass that simply cannot flow through the engine. When this happens engine damage will be immediate if the engine is started without preheating the oil. Oil dipstick heaters can be placed in the oil sump to heat oil but they are not recommended because they are very hot and can be a fire hazard.

Automobile owners have long enjoyed using multiviscosity oils and they are now available for light airplane operators. A multiviscosity oil remains thinner and performs like a lighter weight oil when cold but will not become too thin when heated to normal operating temperatures. For example, a 20-W50 multiviscosity oil will be as thin as normal 20 weight when cold but as thick as normal 50 weight at high temperature. I recommend these oils highly because under all temperatures they will get oil circulating through the engine sooner but not lose lubricating strength when warmed up. Most engines are now approved for multiviscosity use but be sure to check with your shop to be certain your engine can use the new oil.

When you start your engine, especially a cold engine, try to keep rpm as low as possible. Oil will not be circulating immediately so a big blast of high rpm will add extra wear and tear. Low speed start-ups are extremely important in turbocharged engines because high engine speed produces high exhaust pressure across the turbocharger. Engine oil will not effectively reach the turbocharger for a number of seconds at best so very high turbocharger spin speeds can score dry bearings and damage dry oil pressure seals.

Never run your engine faster than 1,000 rpm until you have an indication of oil temperature. Many engines have a yellow band on the oil temperature gauge and cannot be run-up until oil temp is out of the yellow. In my Turbo Arrow, engine speed could not exceed 1,200 rpm until oil temperature was at least 100 degrees F. and on a cold day that would require 10 minutes or more.

Whenever you are taxiing or holding on the ground try to

keep engine rpm near 1,000 because very low idle speeds of 500 or 600 rpm will foul spark plugs. Compared to the damage high engine speeds after start-up can do, spark plug fouling is not serious but it can be avoided. Very slow idle speeds allow internal cylinder temperatures to drop and lead in the fuel can quickly deposit on the spark plugs, shorting out electrodes. During runup a fouled plug will show up as rough running on one mag. One way to clear plugs is to lean the mixture as you run the engine at a medium speed of about 1,500 rpm. Leaning increases internal cylinder temperature and can burn away plug-fouling lead. Be careful not to keep the mixture lean for more than 30 seconds or temperatures could become too high and cause damage.

All takeoffs and initial climbs should be made at full power for obvious performance reasons and to protect your engine. Most fuel systems, either injected or carbureted, enrich the mixture at full power to help cool the cylinders with extra fuel. If you back the throttle off a little, this extra-rich mixture will be lost and you will be harming your engine, not helping it.

After reaching a safe altitude, reduce power as recommended. Many larger engines have two different horsepower ratings, one for takeoff and the other for a continuous maximum power setting. A maximum takeoff rating is usually limited to 5 minutes of operation before manifold pressure and rpm must be reduced. However, if your engine is rated for continuous maximum power, it may be a good idea not to reduce power after takeoff. By keeping the throttles fully advanced, your engine receives the extra-rich takeoff mixture and runs cooler. Maximum power results in a faster climb and as you climb, power is reduced automatically by the lowering ambient air pressure. I believe it is actually less wearing on an engine to climb at maximum continuous power, get to cruise altitude sooner, and benefit from the rich takeoff mixture all through the climb. The engine will work harder for a more brief period and will always be within its operating limits.

This technique does not apply to turbocharged engines because manifold pressure will remain constant in the climb. You can still climb at maximum continuous rated horsepower but the engine will be working at maximum effort all through the climb, not just for the first two thousand feet as a normally aspirated engine would. It is vital that every manufacturer's recommended

The lower corner of the blades on this turbocharger turbine have been eaten away, probably because turbine inlet temperature limits were exceeded. The turbine could have overheated as a result of too lean a mixture or because it was not cooled properly after landing.

procedure be followed with a turbocharged engine and that the pilot closely monitor temperatures during climb. Many turbocharged engines are rated for continuous maximum power climbs but on a hot day that may not be possible without exceeding cylinder head or oil temperatures.

Selecting a cruise power that provides both fuel efficiency and long engine life is no easy task. The most fuel efficient power setting for many light airplanes will be about 55 per cent or slightly less of maximum horsepower. This setting is called best economy and will result in the greatest number of miles flown for each gallon of fuel burned. However, this is usually a rather slow cruise speed, requiring considerably more time to cover a given distance.

The hidden flaw in best economy cruise is engine overhaul expense versus fuel cost. The object of flight, other than for training, is to cover a specific distance, not spend a specific amount of time in the air. As airplane owners we want to fly for the lowest possible cost per mile and that is not always the same as the lowest possible cost per hour.

For example, the Cessna Cutlass RG at 55 per cent power cruises at 117 knots and burns 46 pounds of fuel per hour, while at 65 per cent power, it cruises at 129 knots and uses 53 pounds of fuel per hour. If we divide fuel burn by speed, we find that for each mile flown at 55 per cent the Cutlass will use 0.39 pounds of fuel but only 0.41 pounds of fuel at 65 per cent power. Because the Cutlass is 10 per cent faster at 65 per cent cruise compared to 55 per cent, you will also save that percentage of engine TBO, oil changes, and other hourly maintenance for an extra 5 per cent of fuel burn.

Not every airplane will be like the Cutlass and for some airplanes low power settings may save enough fuel so that the slight speed gain of higher power will not offset fuel savings. However, look at your performance manual and calculate fuel, engine reserves, and other hourly operating expense in miles, not by the hour. I believe you will find most light airplanes operate most efficiently at 65 to 70 per cent power, not the so-called best economy setting of 55 per cent or less. Fuel economy is important and will grow in importance as prices rise, but engine overhaul, oil changes, and 100-hour inspections are also expensive and if you can get more miles per hour you are saving on those costs.

In cruise, leaning is vital to achieve optimum economy and engine life. There is only one optimum fuel-air ratio for each engine and the density of air will change with altitude and temperature. We cannot control air density, so to obtain the correct fuel mixture we must reduce fuel flow to lean the air-fuel mixture.

The best way to adjust mixture in any airplane is with an exhaust temperature gauge (EGT), sometimes called an economy gauge. The EGT measures the temperature of exhaust leaving one or more cylinders and that temperature is directly related to the fuel-air mixture. A leaner mixture containing less fuel burns hotter, a richer mixture of fuel burns cooler.

To use an EGT, reduce the fuel mixture until the temperature reaches a peak. When a mixture is leaned beyond optimum, exhaust temperature will decline because the mixture is too lean to fire properly. When you see the EGT start to drop as you lean, peak has been passed and the mixture must be richened slightly.

Many engines, especially those made by Lycoming, can be operated at peak EGT at cruise power and this provides the best economy mixture. Maximum leaning on other engines is usually 25 degrees rich of peak EGT.

Another mixture setting is called best power, usually 100 degrees rich of peak. At this setting the engine produces the most power for given manifold pressure and rpm. Best power settings will use considerably more fuel while increasing cruise speed only a slight amount. I do not see any good reason to operate at best power mixture unless you are at maximum cruise power setting and wish to go a little bit faster. Best power uses a lot more fuel for very little gain.

There are still a lot of horror stories told in hangars about engine damage caused by too lean a mixture but we should all ignore that talk. If your engine is approved for peak EGT cruise, you will not damage it by operating in that manner. As with all other aspects of flying the manufacturer's recommendations are based on engineering data, not legend, and we cannot go wrong by following recommended procedures.

Leaning an engine without an EGT is not as precise but should still be done. The procedure is to lean until the engine runs rough, indicating it has gone past peak EGT, and then richen the mixture until the engine smooths out. Don't be afraid that you will hurt the engine. As long as you have richened the mixture for smooth operation, you will not damage the engine.

Steady cruise flight is the least wearing type of engine operation. Temperatures are stable, power changes are minimal, and there are no shocks to the engine. When it is time to descend it is important to change the engine from its steady cruise state to a reduced temperature and power operation as gradually as possible. Plan descents to allow time to get down with rather high power settings to keep temperatures stable. I find with good planning it is possible to descend in many airplanes at cruise power settings and still keep airspeed below the VNO yellow mark on the airspeed indicator.

If it is not possible to descend at high speeds because of rough air or if ATC demands a rapid descent rate, one way to get down quickly with high power settings is to extend the landing gear. Most retractable gear add enough drag when extended to achieve at least a 1,000 foot per minute descent with cruise power settings. Obviously, this technique will do little for fixed gear airplane pilots but virtually all airplanes have flaps which can be extended to speed descent.

After landing, turbocharged engines demand a few extra minutes to cool off. The turbocharger wheel will be spinning at very high rpm until the engine is slowed to idle speed so it is important to allow time for the turbo to slow down. By keeping engine rpm at 1,000 or below during taxi, exhaust pressure will be low enough to allow the turbine to slow. If engine power is cut while the turbine is at high speed, it will continue to coast to a stop without pressure lubricating oil from the engine and bearing damage will result. If you have only a short taxi to the ramp, idle the engine for a couple of minutes before shutdown to protect that expensive turbine.

Optimum engine life can only be achieved through regular operation. If you fly your airplane infrequently and less than 200 hours a year total, don't expect the engine to reach manufacturer's recommended TBO before problems occur. Lack of operation allows acids to build up in engine oil. These acids plus other corrosive chemicals attack internal parts of an engine as it sits. Only frequent flights of at least once a week can keep the engine dried out and acid free.

If you find it impossible to fly your airplane regularly, change oil more frequently than recommended. It is worth the money to change engine oil every three months even if you have not flown the normal recommended time, usually 50 hours for a modern engine. More frequent changes will help keep oil from breaking down and should drain out water and acids which built up when the airplane was at rest.

Proper engine operation is the most effective way to save maintenance costs but there are other procedures that can make your airplane last longer, too. Cleanliness is about the most important aspect of all preventive maintenance. Dirt holds moisture, leading to corrosion and deterioration. It is impossible to inspect dirty components for cracks or wear visually. Keeping all parts of the airplane clean will make it last longer and worth more when you sell.

The exterior of an airplane can be cleaned with any of the

popular automotive products. There are many waxes on the market with all manner of claims for durability and shine but I do not know of any that outshines the competition. Any high quality wax will protect airplane exteriors, no matter if the finish is applied to fabric or metal.

Cleaning the plexiglass used for airplane windows and windshields does require special care to avoid scratching. Never use glass cleaners because many products contain solvents strong enough to soften the plexiglass slightly and allow scratching. Never wipe an airplane window with a dry cloth because dirt and dust particles will be rubbed against the surface and cause tiny scratches. Use only those polish and cleaning compounds designed specifically for airplane windows. Plexiglass cleaner contains a very fine abrasive which polishes the surface and waxes that can fill tiny scratches to help preserve transparency.

The working life of tires can be extended by keeping them properly inflated and by protecting them from the sun. Sun damages rubber rapidly so landing gear tires often require replacement because of rubber failure rather than tread wear. Small cracks in the tire sidewall are the usual indications of rot and the best way to avoid this problem is to protect the tires with wheel pants or keep the airplane inside.

Tie-down ropes or chains can cause considerable airframe damage if too much slack is allowed to flap around in the breeze. Even a rather lightweight rope can chip paint or dent aluminum skin if allowed to flog against the airplane. Be sure to secure the loose ends of all tie-downs.

It is an old saw that you should never force anything on an airplane but it is amazing how much damage is done by owners to their own airplanes. Broken door handles from slamming the door, broken knobs on the instrument panel, and all manner of other problems can be created by pilots getting too rough for the lightweight construction of many airplane latches, knobs, and controls.

Even careful pilots can unknowingly cause damage to vernier engine controls by twisting the knob after the control is full forward. When you advance a vernier throttle, mixture, or prop control, push it full forward with the center button depressed but don't twist the vernier portion of the control. Those last little twists when the control is full in will soon break the control.

Perhaps the most effective maintenance cost saving step we can take is to be observant. Remember—if not record, engine gauge readings. Listen for unusual sounds from the engine, airframe, landing gear, or avionics. Keep track of oil consumption and note any change. Pay attention to climb and cruise performance and after adjustment for atmospheric conditions note any changes not caused by weight of the airplane. All of these factors will provide early warning of a pending problem and the sooner you can take symptoms to a qualified shop the less you can expect a repair to cost. Not only will you save money, you may save your life because airplanes almost never fail without at least some advance warnings. Pilot alertness and proper aircraft maintenance all lead to hours and hours of safe and pleasurable flying.

The vernier controls on this Bonanza can be easily damaged if they are twisted all the way into the stop. To move throttle, prop, and mixture controls full forward for takeoff, push in but do not twist. That last little twist against the stop will soon break the control.

Author Biography

J. Mac McClellan is technical editor in charge of avionics and power plant technology for *Flying* magazine. He has won three Aviation Space Writers Association awards for articles on weather radar and avionics maintenance. Before joining the magazine, Mr. McClellan served as a technical writer for the Collins Avionics Division of Rockwell International in Cedar Rapids, Iowa.

Mr. McClellan's writing experience comes primarily from six years as a sports writer for *The Lake County News-Herald,* where he was named Ohio Sports Writer of the Year by the Associated Press.

Index

A

A&P mechanics, 3–4, 116
Accessories problem (during a major overhaul), 112–13
AD Notes, *see* Airworthiness Directive Notification
Aeronca Champ, bungee cords on, 54
AIM, 22
Airframe and power plant (A&P), 3–4, 19
Airframes
  applying preservative material to, 75–77
  logbook, 38, 39
  maintenance problems, 118–28
    control surface, 123–25
    dealing with cracks, 119–20
    fighting corrosion, 120–23
    hangaring decision, 127–28
    landing gear, 125–26
  riveting patches or doubler plates, 78–80
Air-oil gear struts, 55–59
  adding oil, 58
  drawback to servicing, 56–57
  proper inflation value, 57–58
  use of nitrogen, 58, 59
Airplane seats, repair or replacement of, 77–78, 83
Airport approach charts, 22
Air traffic control system, 129
Airworthiness Directive Notification (AD Notes), 31, 83, 142–49
  and buying a used airplane, 147–49
  containing diagrams directing inspection and repair, 146
  development of, 142–43
  emergency, 145
  increase in, 147
  ownership of records, 146–47
  paying for the work, 147
  published, 145–46
  purpose of, 142
  research service for, 148–49
  sources of information leading to, 144–45
Altimeters, hysteresis in, 23
Altimeter test, 23–24
Aluminum corrosion, 121
A-N fittings, 94

Annual inspection, 2–18, 32, 35, 37, 39, 100, 123
A&P mechanic for, 3–4
brakes, 15–16
complexity of, 4
engine, 4–14, 17–18
compression check, 4–8
fuel system and carburetor, 11–14
ignition system, 8–11
run-up, 17–18
flight performance, 18
IA rating, 4
list of defects found, 42–43
lube job, 17
oil squirt, 18
plates and vital components, 3
propeller, 14–15
purpose of, 18
tires and wheels, 15
way to avoid, 19–20
A-N rivets, 78
Anticollision lights, repair of, 85
ATC contact, 129
Authorized inspector (IA), 3
Autopilots, 139
Avionics, 129–41
building a system, 137–41
buying used, 141
decision between factory-installed and field installation, 140
electrical power used in, 130–31
heat problems, 130–33
installation, 139–40
meaning of, 129
moisture-fighting techniques, 133–35
package, 130, 132
reported a failure, 135–37
warranty, 141
Avco Lycoming, guaranteed horsepower output program, 7

B

Batteries
repair shop stocking of, 29
replacing and servicing, 96–97
Battery acid, 96, 97
Beacon failure, 86
Beechcraft Bonanza model 35 series, 28
Beech 18 wing spar, AD Notes against, 143
Bilge cleaning, 121–22
Blade failures, 115–16
nicks or cracks, 14–15
Blade tip clip, 117
Bonanza series, cowlings on, 87
Brake caliper, 50
Brake disk, 50
Brake disk rust, 15, 16, 17
Brake pads, repair shop stocking of, 29
Brake piston O-ring, 17
Brakes
annual inspection of, 15–16
hydraulic fluid leaks, 16, 17
O-ring failure, 17
Bungee cords, 53–54, 55
Business and Commercial Aviation (magazine), 111

C

Cable tension, 124
Caliper mechanism, dirt and, 16
Cessna 182, oil change on, 67

Cessna 337, inspection plate on underside of, 3
Chafe problem, 124
Chrome molly steel tubing, protective coating for, 76–77
Civil Aeronautics Authority, 142
Cleanliness, repair shop, 29
Climate, hangaring decision and, 127–28
Component cracking, 120
Compression check, 4–8
  break-in period, 6
  pressure, 4–5
  worn valve stems, 8
  written results, 7
Compression test, 5
Conquest aircraft, AD grounding of, 143
Control cables, corrosion problems, 121
Control hinges
  lubricating, 68–69
  wear and resultant slop in, 125
Controllable pitch props, 14, 15
Control surfaces, 118–19
  maintenance problems, 123–25
Cord installation, 53–55
Corrosion, airframe, 118
  fighting, 120–23
Cotter keys, replacing, 62–65
  first step in, 65
  how to begin, 63–64
  safetyed to a primary structure, 64–65
Cowlings, replacing without removing propeller, 87–89
Cracks, airframe, 118
  dealing with, 119–20
Cracks, repairing, 78–80
Crashes, causes of, 143
Cruise power, fuel efficiency and, 154–55
Cylinders, 101–2
  compression leak, 5–6
  decision on rebuilding or replacing, 104–5
  major repairs, 111
  top overhaul of, 101–6
    logbook entry, 106
    objections to, 105–6

D

Dacron, 127
Decals, 78
Decorative coating, refinishing, 74–75
Dents, repairing, 78–80
Department of Transportation (DOT), 24
Detergent oil, 116
DME, 129, 135
  integration with an RNAV, 137–38
Dope paint finish, 128
Doubler plates, riveting, 78–80

E

Elastic shock absorbers, replacing, 53–55
Emergency AD, 145
Engine
  annual inspection, 4–14, 17–18
    compression check, 4–8

exhaust system, 11–12
fuel system and carburetor, 11–14
harness (spark plug wires), 8–9
ignition system, 8–11
magnetos, 8
oil, 12–13
rated horsepower, 7
run-up, 17–18
spark plugs, 8, 9–11
"staking" the valve, 6
"tune-up" phase, 8
wash down, 13–14, 68
logbooks, 39
maintenance records, 39
100-hour inspections, 19
rated horsepower, 7
repair and overhaul, 100–17
concept of TBO, 100–1, 105, 107, 108, 113, 114
major overhauls, 107–17
top overhaul, 101–7
safe and saving operating techniques, 152–58
best power settings, 156
cruise power and fuel efficiency, 154–55
descent rate, 156–57
exhaust temperature gauge (EGT), 155–56
leaning without EGT, 156
maximum power, 153–54
starting up, 152–53
takeoffs and initial climb, 153
taxiing or holding on the ground, 152–53
turbocharged, 153–54
Engine hour meters, 40
Engine valve covers, 7
Exhaust pipe cracks, 12
Exhaust systems
cracks or blown exhaust gaskets, 12
metal alloy used in, 11
vibration in, 12
Exhaust temperature gauge (EGT), 155–56
Exhaust valve compression leaks, 6
Exterior protective coating, 75–77
Exterior window covers, 134

F

FAA, 1, 3, 4, 19, 21, 22, 23–24, 32
AD Notes, 31, 142, 143, 144–45, 146, 147
maintenance records and, 36, 37, 38, 41, 42, 43, 44
major overhauls and, 111, 112, 113, 116
owner-pilot preventive maintenance, 45–46, 51, 57, 72, 74, 75–76, 83, 84, 90, 98
FAA/GADO (General Aviation District Officer), 144, 148
Fabric patches, 70–72
Factory rebuilt engines, 112
Factory school certificates, 27
Fail-safe design concept, 36–37
FBO, 21
Federal Air Regulations (FARs), 1, 34, 36, 43, 119
major overhauls and, 108
owner-pilot preventive maintenance and, 50, 51, 53, 55–57, 59, 61, 62, 65, 70, 74, 85, 87, 89
Federal Register, 145–46

Fiber glass repair, 80–81
Fine wire spark plugs, 10–11, 90–91
Fixed pitch props, 14
Flange crack, exhaust stack, 12
Flaps, lubricating, 70
Flight control system, avionics planning, 138–39
Flight performance, inspection of, 18
Fowler-type flaps, 70
Fuel injection metering systems, 11
Fuel prices, xv
Fuel strainers, cleaning, 95–96
Fuel system and carburetor, 11–14
Fuselage belly, corrosion problems, 121
Fuselage formers, corrosion problems, 121

G

GADO, *see* FAA/GADO (General Aviation District Office)
Gliders, assembling, 97–99
Goodyear brakes, floating disk on, 50–51
Grease, 15, 61, 126
Grease fittings, lubricating, 125

H

Hangaring decision, 127–28
Harness, annual inspection of, 8–9
Hinges, lubricating, 123, 125
Hired planes, 100-hour inspection of, 19
Hobbs meter, 40
Horizontal Situation Indicator (HSI), 132, 137, 138
Horsepower, 7
Hoses, replacing, 93–94
Hour meters, best way to install, 40–41
HSI, *see* Horizontal Situation Indicator
Hub, speed prop, 115
Hydraulic fluid, replenishing, 72–74
Hydraulic fluid leaks, 16, 17
Hysteresis, 23

I

IA, *see* Inspection authorization rating
IFR, 1, 20, 22, 23, 93, 129
Ignition system, annual inspection of, 8–11
Incoder, 24
Injector nozzles, 11
Inner tubes, tire change, 51
Inspection authorization rating (IA), 4, 5, 19, 33, 39, 43, 120, 123, 124, 148
Inspection plates, 3

J

Jack points, 48–49, 50
J-3 Cub, shock-absorbing bungee cords on, 54

J-3 Piper Cub expanding-type brake, 51
Jugs, 101–2

K

King KCS-55A, 138
King Radio, 141
KX 170 and KX 175 navcoms, 141

L

Landing gear, lubricating, 69–70
Landing gear problems, 125–26
Landing lights, replacing, 83–86
Lap seams, sealing, 123
Lightweight oxygen tanks, 24–25
Logbooks, 37–38, 39, 149
Loose-leaf record book, 37, 38
Low oil pressure, 107–8
Lube job, 17
Lubricating oil, 150, 157
Lubrication, 65–70
  control hinges, 68–69
  flaps, 70
  grease fittings, 125
  hinges, 123, 125
  landing gear, 69–70
  oil changing, 65–68
Luscombe (cowling), 87

M

Magnetos
  AD Note for, 147
  annual inspection of, 8
Maintenance records, 36–44
  and buying a used plane, 43–44
  defects found during annual inspection, 42–43
  difference between maintenance and preventive maintenance, 41, 45–46
  fail-safe design concept, 36–37
  length of time for, 38–39
  logbooks, 37–38
  loose-leaf binder, 37, 38
  on major alterations, 42
  need for, 36
  service personnel, 36
  337 forms, 41–42
  total time in service, 39–41
Major overhauls, 107–17
  due to low oil pressure, 107–8
  engine overhaul or exchange shop, 110–12
  FAA and, 111, 112, 113, 116
  factory, 122
  FARs and, 108
  kind of oil to use, 116
  power settings, 116–17
  problems of accessories, 112–13
  propeller work, 113–16
  recommended TBO, 108
  small shop, 108–10
Malfunction and Defect Report, 144
Massive electrode plugs, 10, 11, 90, 91
Mattituck (engine overhaul shop), 111–12
Metal components, cracks in, 120

Mil-H-5606 (hydraulic fluid), 72
Mineral oil, non-detergent, 116
Minimum idle speed, 11
Mode C, 24
Moisture
  as cause of corrosion, 121, 122–23, 126, 127
  in radios, 133–35
Multiviscosity oils, 66, 152

N

National Transporation Safety Board (NTSB), 143
Nav lights, replacing, 83–86
Nicks, propeller, 14–15
Nitrogen, 58, 59

O

OBS, *see* Omni bearing selector
Oil
  after a major overhaul, 116
  air temperature and, 150–51
  annual inspection, 12–13
  changing, 65–68, 150
  leaking from the prop, 15
  multiviscosity, 66, 152
  progressive inspection of, 21
  safe and saving operating techniques, 150–52
  viscosity weight, 66
Oil filters, 68
  full-flow type, 69
Oil screen, cleaning, 68
Oleo struts, servicing, 55–59
  adding oil, 58
  drawback to, 56–57
  proper inflation value, 57–58
  use of nitrogen, 58, 59
Omni bearing selector (OBS), 22
100-hour inspections, 18–20, 21, 37, 39, 43, 100
O-ring failure, 17
Out-of-rig airplane, 124
Owner-pilot preventive maintenance, 45–99
  air-oil (or oleo strut), 55–59
  assembling gliders, 97–99
  battery servicing and replacement, 96–97
  changing from wheels to skis, 86–87
  cleaning fuel and oil strainers, 95–96
  cowling replacement (without removing propeller), 87–89
  elastic shock absorbers, 53–55
  exterior protective coating, 75–77
  FAA regulations, 45–46, 51, 57, 72, 74, 75–76, 83, 84, 90, 98
  fabric patches, 70–72
  FARs and, 50, 51, 53, 55–57, 59, 61, 62, 65, 70, 74, 85, 87, 89
  hose replacement, 93–94
  inspection and, 98–99
  landing lights and Nav lights, 83–86
  lubrication, 65–70
  nonstructural items, 78–81
  refinishing decorative coating, 74–75

replacing refabricated fuel lines, 94
replacing side windows, 81–83
replenishing hydraulic fluid, 72–74
safety belt replacement, 83
safety wire or cotter keys, 62–65
seat replacement, 83
spark plug care, 89–93
tire changes, 48–53
types of, 46–48
upholstery repair or replacement, 77–78
wheel bearings, 59–62
Oxygen tank test, 24–25

P

Painting an airplane, 74–75
Paperwork, *see* Maintenance records
Patches
fabric, 70–72
riveting, 78–80
Piano hinges, 123
Piedmont (engine overhaul shop), 111–12
Piper Archer cowling, removing, 88
Piper Archer engine, magnetos on, 9
Plexiglass, 158
Plexiglass windows, 81
Pop rivets, 78
Power settings, overhaul and, 116–17
Prefabricated fuel lines, replacing, 94
Preventive aircraft maintenance
airframe problems, 118–28
Airworthiness Directives, 31, 83, 142–49
avionics, 129–41
difference between maintenance and, 41, 45–46
engine repair and overhaul, 100–17
introduction to, xv–xvi
owner-pilot, 45–99
quality repair shop (how to identify), 26–35
safe and saving operating techniques, 150–59
scheduled inspection and, 1–25
Progressive inspections, 20–21
Propeller
annual inspection of, 14–15
blade failures, 115–16
maintenance records, 39
major overhauls, 113–16
nicks or cracks on the blade, 14–15
track accuracy, 15
on twin-engine airplanes, 115

Q

Quality maintenance shop (how to identify), 26–35
asking another plane owner, 28–29
cleanliness, 29
dealership operations, 28, 29
diagnosis of the problem, 31
discrepancy sheet listing, 34
display of awards and certificates, 27
estimates, 31–34

factors to keep in mind, 26–27
familiarity with owner's type of plane, 27–29
frequency of owners type of plane in shop, 30–31
hidden maintenance problems, 33–34
library of service literature, 31, 32
posting of rates for inspection, 33
repair charges and, 27
sticking with a good shop, 34–35
stocked parts department, 30
visual examination, 29–30

R

Radar contact loss, 135
Radios, *see* Avionics
Ram air scoop, 131–32
Record keeping, 25
Rental planes, 100-hour inspection of, 19
Retractable landing gear problems, 125–26
lubricating, 69–70
Rig, 124–25
Riveting patches or doubler plates, 78–80
RNAV, 129, 139
Rotation, spark plug, 92–93
Run-up, engine, 17–18

S

SAE aircraft oil, 151
Safe and saving operating techniques, 150–59
best power settings, 156
cleanliness, 157–58
cruise power and fuel efficiency, 154–55
descent rate, 156–57
engine, 152–58
exhaust temperature gauge (EGT), 155–56
extending working life of tires, 158
leaning engine without EGT, 156
lubricating oil, 150, 157
maximum power, 153–54
most effective cost saving step, 159
oil, 150–52
starting the engine, 152–53
takeoffs and initial climbs, 153
taxiing or holding on the ground, 152–53
vernier throttle, 158, 159
with turbocharged engine, 153–54
Safety, xv
Safety belts, replacing, 83
Safety wire, replacing, 62–65
how to begin, 63–64
to a primary structure, 64–65
Scheduled inspection and maintenance, 1–25
annual, 2–18, 32, 35, 37, 39, 100, 123
cost of, 2
100-hour, 18–20, 21, 37, 39, 43, 100
oxygen tank, 24–25
progressive scheme, 20–21
record keeping, 25
responsibility for, 1–2
static system test, 23–24

transponder test, 24
VOR check, 22–23
Schneck (engine overhaul shop), 111–12
Sealed beam lights, 84
Seats, replacing, 77–78, 83
Service award, shop display of, 27
Side windows, replacing, 81–83
Silver Crown equipment, 141
Skis, changing from wheels to, 86–87
Spark plugs, 89–93
annual inspection of, 8, 9–11
blaster and vibrator, 91, 92
categories of, 90–91
repair shop stocking of, 29
replacing, cleaning, and gapping, 89–93
types of, 10–11
Speed props, 114–15
Spring landing gear, 49
Stainless steel control cables, 124
"Staking" the valve, 6
Standard weight oxygen tanks, 24
Static system test, 23–24
Steel tubing, protective coating for, 76–77
Stop-drilling, 119–20
Strainers, cleaning, 95–96
Stringers, corrosion problems, 121
Strobe problems, 85–86
"Sucking a valve," 104
Sunlight, as cause of corrosion, 127
Sunscreens, 133
Surface corrosion, 122

T

Tachometers, 40
Tail surfaces, surface corrosion on, 122
Tail wheel problems, 126
Taxiing or holding on the ground, 152–53
Taxi lights, 84
TBO, *see* Time between overhaul
TCAs, 129
Teledyne Continental, guaranteed horsepower output program, 7
337 form, 41–42, 83, 86
Tie-down ropes or chains, 158
Time between overhaul (TBO), 100–1, 105, 107, 108, 113, 114
Tires
annual inspection of, 15
changes, 48–53
balance, 52
brakes and, 50–51
inner tubes, 51
maintenance shop, 52–53
reinflation, 51–52
extending working life of, 158
repair shop stocking of, 29
Top overhauls, 101–7
cylinders, 101–6
logbook entry, 106
objections to, 105–6
downtime required for, 106–7
as favorite of used airplane salesmen, 107
Torque wrench, 89–90
Track accuracy, propeller, 15
Transponder, buying used, 141

Transponder test, 24
TSO specs, 141
"Tune-up," 8
Turbocharged engines, cool off after landing, 157
Turbocharger systems, 113
Twin-engine airplanes, propellers used on, 115
T. W. Smith (engine overhaul shop), 111–12

U

Ultrasonic testing, 109
Upholstery repair or replacement, 77–78

V

Valve failure, 103
Valve guides, 103–4
Valves, "staking," 6
Velcro tabs, 132
Vernier controls, advancing, 158, 159
VFR, 129
Vibration, exhaust system, 12
VOR accuracy test, 22–23
VOR receivers, 22
VOT test signal, 22

W

Wash down, 13–14, 68
Waxes, 158
Welding, 12
Western Skyways (engine overhaul shop), 111–12
Wheel bearings, 59–62
  checking for water, 60–61
  greasing, 15
  reassembly, 61–62
Wheels
  annual inspection of, 15
  changing to skis, 86–87
Windows, replacing, 81–83
Wings, surface corrosion on, 122
Wiring, corrosion problems, 121
Worn alternator drive belts, 20
Worn cylinder, 5–6
Worn piston rings, 5–6

X

X-ray testing, 109

Z

Zinc chromate primer, 76, 77, 122